ASHE-ERIC Higher Education Report: Volume 30, Number 1
Adrianna J. Kezar, Series Editor

Governance in the Twenty-First-Century University

Approaches to Effective Leadership and Strategic Management

Dennis John Gayle, Bhoendradatt Tewarie, and A. Quinton White, Jr.

Governance in the Twenty-First-Century University: Approaches to Effective Leadership and Strategic Management
Dennis John Gayle, Bhoendradatt Tewarie, A. Quinton White, Jr.
ASHE-ERIC Higher Education Report: Volume 30, Number 1
Adrianna J. Kezar, Series Editor

This publication was prepared partially with funding from the Office of Educational Research and Improvement, U.S. Department of Education, under contract no. ED-99-00-0036. The opinions expressed in this report do not necessarily reflect the positions or policies of OERI or the Department.

ISSN 0884-0040   electronic ISSN 1536-0709   ISBN 0-7879-7174-X

The **ASHE-ERIC Higher Education Report** is part of the Jossey-Bass Higher and Adult Education Series and is published six times a year by Wiley Subscription Services, Inc., A Wiley Company, at Jossey-Bass, 989 Market Street, San Francisco, California 94103-1741.

For subscription information, see the Back Issue/Subscription Order Form in the back of this journal.

CALL FOR PROPOSALS: Prospective authors are strongly encouraged to contact Adrianna Kezar at the University of Southern California, Waite Phillips Hall 703C, Los Angeles, CA 90089, or kezar@usc.edu. See "About the ASHE-ERIC Higher Education Report Series" in the back of this volume.

Visit the Jossey-Bass Web site at **www.josseybass.com.**

Printed in the United States of America on acid-free recycled paper.

Advisory Board

The ASHE-ERIC Higher Education Report Series is sponsored by the Association for the Study of Higher Education (ASHE), which provides an editorial advisory board of ASHE members.

This Issue's Consulting Editors and Review Panelists

Executive Summary

This book explores approaches to effective leadership and strategic management in the twenty-first-century university, using a distinctive entry point: the perceptions and attitudes of university leaders toward the institutional structures and organizational cultures within which we lead and manage our universities, together with the implications of these attitudes for the central concerns of higher education. After reviewing the historical educational environment within which university governance evolved, we discuss twenty-first-century demands on governance, primarily but not exclusively in the United States of America. These demands include greater student access to educational opportunities, a key source of legislative, system, and trustee expectations for expanded accountability. In the higher education environment, public funding has been significantly reduced, encouraging the emergence of academic entrepreneurs working alongside teacher-scholars in a context of increasingly diffuse authority. At the same time, the evolution of distance education, from correspondence courses to e-learning networks, has added to the pressures acting on governance in higher education. These factors are changing the higher education landscape as well as traditional perceptions of governance at a previously unimaginable rate.

Such change leads to several instrumental questions: How are governance systems most effectively structured, and how is the interplay of organizational culture, institutional mission, and university governance structure best specified? What exactly is the difference between managing universities in a businesslike manner and treating universities as businesses, or between education and training? What kinds of institutional leadership will best address the challenges discussed? The stage is thus set for a return to the concerns posed by competing perspectives and expectations on the part of university stakeholders. Based on content analysis of the literature, we identify three core governance-related issues for further discussion: teaching and learning, information technology and distance education, resource allocation and accountability. The conclusion recapitulates the key findings of this work regarding university leadership and management, provides a new model of governance structure and process, and explains what policy directions readers might want to carry away. Only real difficulties can be overcome, whereas imaginary ones remain insuperable. The conclusion further clarifies the rationales for our initial suggestions with the aid of several flexible frames of reference. Improved communication naturally remains a key imperative. This work is rooted in both realist and pragmatic approaches to the internal and external institutional environment. The goal is to encourage and assist higher education leaders to do all we can, where we are, with what we have to improve the quality of governance in higher education institutions. We take a practical view of things, examining the realities, assessing their implications, and suggesting possible ways forward.

In examining the evolving structure and process of governance in the twenty-first-century university, we take a three-pronged approach. First, we examine the literature on the state of university governance. This examination primarily focuses on those issues that bear on higher education leadership and management, technology, teaching and learning, and budgeting, given their centrality for higher education. The overview includes a discussion of the key concepts, issues, and indicators that impact the effectiveness of governance systems.

Second, we recognize that the first step toward effective change is at least emerging consensus among leading constituents that change is needed. Consequently, we review several surveys of faculty leaders and administrators, explore trustees' perspectives and discuss inferences drawn from a range of minicases, including those from George Mason, Adelphi, Dubuque, Hollins, Auburn, Florida International, Toledo, and Southern Mississippi Universities. This approach enables us to better understand observations and perceptions regarding governance issues, and to recognize coherent patterns across governance models, constraints on, and opportunities for fundamental governance reform.

Third, we identify sources of continuing conflicts in attitudes toward governance, inside and outside the academy, taking into account interests of various stakeholders. A better understanding of prime stakeholders' perceptions—compatible and conflicting alike—is a requisite condition for devising improved governance models. Yet understanding is necessarily incomplete when issues are examined from one perspective or by a single audience (Kezar and Eckel, 2000). Finally, it is our hope that the reference list serve as a basis for future studies of university governance and reviews of possible further research directions.

Contents

Foreword

In recent years, the higher education literature has been filled with calls for institutions to respond to a myriad of changes in technology, student demographics, globalization, and declining funding, to name a few. Moreover, almost every part of the institution has been affected. Curricular innovations include community service–learning. Assessment has altered the character of administrative work. New notions of scholarship have expanded the role of faculty. Changes in core functions—teaching—and roles—faculty contracts—are becoming part of the academy. Yet the character of academic governance has changed very little.

Certainly, calls for change have been sounded over the past few decades, including Keller's suggestion (1983) to develop joint big decision committees to make more strategic decisions or Benjamin and Carroll's recommendation (1998) to redesign and restructure campus governance to be more responsive and less bureaucratic. Trustees, policymakers, and administrators are becoming more concerned that governance processes are no longer functional and cannot carry out the work of contemporary institutions. Yet little change in the structure or process of governance has occurred.

Some trustees, legislatures, and higher education associations suggest that academic governance limits an institution's agility and flexibility, creates obstructions, sluggishness, and inefficiency, and fosters a predisposition toward the status quo. Some campus leaders are reported to be bypassing traditional academic governance structures or substituting corporate approaches to make quick changes. But supporters of traditional academic governance believe that the distinctive dynamics (consensus building and dialogue) are what help institutions arrive at better, more thoroughly examined conclusions. Supporters of traditional governance worry that administrators have become fixated on meeting political and social pressures for finances, efficiency, and accountability and have lost touch with education-based decision making, quality, and the real purposes of higher education. Tension is growing between traditional academic governance and corporate approaches to decision making, with most commentators concluding that neither approach in its current form will successfully meet the challenges of today's environment.

This new ASHE-ERIC monograph helps to move past this stalemate of views, seeking an alternative perspective that incorporates both critics' and supporters' perspectives of traditional governance. Dennis J. Gayle, Bhoendradatt Tewarie, and A. Quinton White set the context for this complex discussion by describing how changes in the environment directly affect governance and then developing a detailed analysis of the reasons governance may need to be altered. They present an overview of the literature on the state of university governance, focusing primarily on leadership and management, technology, teaching and learning, and budgeting. The authors focus on the relationship of governance to teaching and learning; one of their primary assumptions is that governance structures should be continually evaluated from the perspective of their contribution toward the strengthening of a learning culture.

A key insight of this monograph is that faculty, administrators, and trustees tend to see and understand governance differently. These differences are traced through empirical data and revealed through surveys. These distinctive beliefs are a significant part of why governance structures have not evolved. As the authors note, "Actual or potential clashes among academic, political, and corporate cultures only further increase the difficulty of addressing university governance structures. . . . University trustees, administrators, and faculty leaders continue to exemplify differential perspectives on the scope of their respective authority and responsibility."

In conclusion, the authors argue that "there is no substitute for community dialogue that includes trustees, administrators, faculty, and students about the relationship between teaching, research, and governance structure. Yet leaders must also be prepared to find that such dialogue might reveal new differences in attitudes and values that might not have been previously anticipated but need to be addressed." They also suggest a new model for governance in the twenty-first century. This decentralized model that builds on earlier scholars' work places various expectations and values of stakeholders at the center. Without some agreement and discussion, no governance process can be functional. The model also relies heavily on authentic leadership and the effective use of technology. The ideas presented in this model help constituents of the governance process to reenvision their work.

Adrianna J. Kezar
Series Editor

Acknowledgments

I wish to acknowledge the excellent advice and support unstintingly given by my host and mentor, former President Patricia Ewers of Pace University, as well as the many helpful suggestions made by several other 1997–1998 ACE fellows, particularly Toufic M. Hakim, Vijendra K. Agarwal, and Peter J. Alfonso. This work was significantly informed by the unique opportunity to discuss institutional structures and strategic plans in relation to the higher education environment with many presidents, vice presidents, and other university and system leaders during invited visits to more than thirty universities in the United States and Australia as part of my ACE fellowship. The editorial assistance of Bernadette E. Warner and Sophia F. Gayle was invaluable. I benefited from the thoughtful comments of several colleagues and the incisive insights of Richard Chait during my participation in Harvard University's 2001 Institute of Educational Management and a seminar dealing with educational entrepreneurship. (Dennis J. Gayle)

I wish to express sincere thanks to the chancellor of the University of the West Indies, Sir Shridath Ramphal, and the vice chancellor, the Honorable Rex Nettleford, for their support and guidance, especially during my first year in office as pro vice-chancellor and campus principal. I wish also to thank senior management and the deans and heads of departments who have given unstinting support in operationalizing the university's 2002–2007 strategic plan at St. Augustine. Sincere thanks are also due to the board of directors and the management and staff of the Institute of Business of the University of the West Indies's St. Augustine campus in Trinidad, where I first had the opportunity to consider and experiment with issues of governance in a higher education institution. (Bhoendradatt Tewarie)

I wish to gratefully acknowledge the support and encouragement of Jesse S. Robertson, former vice president for academic affairs, and Joan Carver, former dean of arts and sciences, at Jacksonville University, and the wise counsel of Gerald Francis, provost and vice president for academic affairs at Elon University. Their reflections on shared governance were extraordinarily helpful, as were the comments of other 1997–1998 colleagues during my experience as a fellow of the American Council on Education. (A. Quinton White)

Introduction

WHAT ARE THE FORCES that influence university governance in the twenty-first century, and how do university leaders seek to respond? Let us begin by defining such governance. University governance refers to the structure and process of authoritative decision making across issues that are significant for external as well as internal stakeholders within a university. Effective governance provides institutional purpose, clarifies strategic direction, identifies priorities, and exerts sufficient control to manage outcomes. The attitudes and values of individual leaders, together with the underlying organizational culture, are at least as important for governance as institutional structure. Successful governance, however, also depends on the extent of agreement concerning institutional mission and the degree of consensus as to the implications of institutional culture. It may also become a means of retarding, if not halting, undesired institutional change until internal conversations concerning goals and objectives, given the nature of the environment, encourage the necessary adjustments in direction. Often there is an interplay of forces within a university, which, in favorable circumstances, can facilitate productive internal exchanges, dialogues, and debates concerning goals and objectives in the context of a particular environment. In turn, this can facilitate agreement on action and strengthen the governance structure of the institution.

The structure of university governance may be visualized in several ways, for example, as a series of concentric circles or as a set of overlapping circles. In any case, an extensive group of stakeholders seek to influence university rules and policies in the United States. These stakeholders include higher education associations, funding organizations, the U.S. Department of

Education, related congressional committees, accrediting institutions, system-level offices, governors, state departments or boards of education, state legislators, students, alumni, local community members, trustees, senior administrators, faculty leaders, and presidents. In other countries, the names or labels of the stakeholders may change, but the variety of stakeholders involved, the power and influence that they wield, and their significance and value to the university as an institution remain about the same.

We posit that universities and their governance systems have been subject to break-point change since the early 1980s, when neoliberalism became the global economic orthodoxy. Multinational corporations, intracorporate trade, and intercorporate trade assumed greater salience in the global economy as communications and transport technologies made distance an increasingly unimportant factor. The World Trade Organization, replacing the General Agreement on Tariffs and Trade, joined the International Monetary Fund and the World Bank in a Washington Consensus underpinning trade and financial liberalization, together with privatization, deregulation, and a marked reduction in the economic role of governments as accepted international norms. The demand for flexible and adaptable knowledge workers and the speed of economic change expanded as information itself became an increasingly critical production factor. Yet knowledge also tended to be more specialized than ever before as interest in cross-disciplinary research expanded, requiring more and more work across disciplinary and departmental boundaries (Ewell, 1997).

As the twentieth century ended, institutions of higher education were challenged by declining public investment, growing criticism of management in the academy and elevated tuition costs, demands for new measures and methods of accountability, unprecedented advances in instructional and communications technology, competition from for-profit providers, increased faculty and student mobility across international borders, and the expanded exports of educational programs and services (Ward, 2003). As a result, universities have been forced to make strategic choices concerning their competitive edges in both teaching and research, while placing an unprecedented premium on institutional flexibility. For instance, in April 2000, Fairleigh Dickinson University set out to operationalize a new mission statement with the goal of preparing students to function effectively in an environment characterized by diversity, global interrelationships, extensive digital information access, and rapid change.

In many countries, a combination of rapidly growing demand for access to higher education and limited capacity has led to increased tuition and other costs for students, while driving publicly funded institutions to seek expanded revenue flows by entrepreneurial activities at home and abroad, including distance education and the establishment of host country campuses. At the same time, public universities are requesting more autonomy from government regulation in the interests of greater flexibility, and a growing number of private universities are entering the market. Indeed, the application of the General Agreement on Trade in Services (GATS) to higher education has generated new controversies regarding the meaning of most-favored nation, national treatment, transparency, mechanisms for settling disputes, monopolies, quality assurance, accreditation, and the role of government in education.

The articulated U.S. position on the application of GATS to higher education is that private education will continue to supplement, not displace, public education systems. Skeptics continue to argue that the expansion of cross-border educational services, typically from advanced industrial to developing countries, is likely to challenge efforts to formulate and implement national education objectives, including the preservation of cultural identity and academic quality rather than revenue potential as a superordinate goal (Knight, 2002). It is also instructive that those pressing for the application of GATS to higher education tend to be motivated by potential profit rather than educational opportunities; several U.S. educational organizations, including the American Council on Education and the Council on Higher Education Accreditation, have strong reservations, contending that GATS encourages universities to emphasize commercialization rather than their core missions of teaching, research, and service, and their contributions to sustainable development and civil society (Altbach, 2002, p. 16).

Across national higher education sectors, however, the scope of stakeholders' demands for access, quality assurance, and government regulation has significantly expanded. Education itself became a significant growth industry, essential to support the requirements and demands of the information age. Today, advanced educational technologies have become more and more ubiquitous. Knowledge, if not necessarily wisdom and understanding, continues to increase at an exponential rate. For instance, the number of scientific articles published in scholarly journals is now doubling almost every fifteen years.

In the United States, for-profit institutions such as the University of Phoenix constitute the most rapidly growing sector of higher education, even as a wave of consolidation has washed over smaller companies in this sector. More graduating high school students than ever before seek admission to colleges and universities, while almost every college is spending more than it charges to educate undergraduates. Traditional students, those from eighteen to twenty-three years of age, are increasingly a minority of the total student population. Inflation-adjusted growth in public sector funding of higher education has ended, even as legislators and governors require greater accountability and curricular relevance. The changing environment of higher education in the United States is also reflected in other areas of the world as globalization spreads, the knowledge economy becomes a reality, and universities everywhere are forced to meet the challenges of information technology and distance education, resource allocation and accountability, and the need for reassessing the teaching and learning environment.

In this climate, there is a growing consensus that university governance structures require significant adjustment; the question is in what ways, through what sequence, and by whom? (See Astin, 1993; Rosenzweig, 1994; Healy, 1997; Tierney, 1998; Hakim, Gayle, Agarwal, and Alfonso, 1999.) Yet how seriously can universities pursue change when fundamental decisions about the essence of a university have to be confronted. For example, should traditional universities emulate for-profit institutions by competitively eliminating unprofitable courses and slashing services to disadvantaged students? And given that shared governance is frequently advocated and accepted as desirable, should a university completely operationalize mutual interdependence among students, faculty, staff, administrators, and trustees when full application of this concept is more than likely to slow the rate of required change? Curricular matters present a particularly significant flash point, because faculty tend to regard the management of such issues as a core prerogative, whereas trustees typically see the need to approve all major instructional program offerings, given their implications for the mission and finances of any university (Committee T on College and University Government, 1964; Dykes, 1970; Floyd, 1994; Dickeson, 1999). Actual or potential clashes among academic, political, and corporate cultures only further increase the difficulty of addressing university governance structures. Meanwhile, academic entrepreneurs coexist with traditional teacher-scholars. University trustees, administrators, and faculty leaders continue to exemplify differential perspectives on the scope of their respective authority and responsibility.

The directions in which and rapidity with which the higher education environment is changing suggest that all university leaders have a common stake in the reform of governance systems. It may be clearest in the intensity of the debates regarding the relative weights applied to teaching and research and the utility of information technology in enhancing student enrollments and retention. These debates have generated questions concerning identity, purpose, and market positioning, in many cases without necessarily fostering climates of civility and trust between higher education leaders, including faculty, administrators, and trustees. Yet such a climate is essential to successful change.

Some observers have projected the advent of what has been termed *the new university,* which would use information technology effectively to promote decentralized responsibility, accountability, authority, and inclusiveness while creating governance systems that can set priorities, focus missions, and implement choices rather than simply identify winners and losers at any given time. Distinctions between traditional residential universities *(brick),* for-profit institutions *(click),* and *brick-and-click* universities remain relevant (Levine, 1997), as do the categories *public* and *private* universities, although both increasingly seek support from private donors as well as state and federal governments. Further, both can collaborate to advance public as well as private purposes as exemplified by customized research undertaken by public research universities and subsidized by private corporations, or customized worker training at community colleges or within colleges of continuing education. There remains the challenge of encouraging adequate public investment in higher education, even as the viability of private alternatives at least potentially diminishes the willingness to make such investments.

As the higher education environment continues to evolve, questions emerge more rapidly than responses can be developed. Will at least some faculty entrepreneurs no longer need universities, as other faculty members assume roles analogous to mentors, or course facilitators, or teaching assistants? Alternatively, will significant numbers of faculty become sought-after designers of effective learning experiences rather than traditional teachers? Will faculty sovereignty over the curriculum diminish to the point where clients will designate both required content and desired instructor? Will a few hundred small liberal arts colleges, community colleges, large research universities, and online institutions, with widely recognized brand names and access to investor capital, eventually provide most education and training in America? And if these brand name institutions have unrestricted access to the best and wealthiest students in the world, what would be the likely implications of such a development?

The concept of *university* may itself become an issue with regard to university governance. From a historical perspective, the word *university* may be traced to the corporate structure of the medieval guild—tenure itself being a doctrine of medieval law that emerged as a means of protecting the freehold rights of nobles and clergy to land and public office against royal assertions of privilege. More recently, although some may emphasize the discovery, transmission, and application of knowledge in communities of scholars and teachers as core university functions, others may focus on issues related to economics, budgets, and market responsiveness. Some may even view the institution as an ordered sociopolitical community that must constantly make distinctions between ideas, on the one hand, and individual achievements, on the other. In such cases, trustees, administrators, and faculty need to work creatively within particular organizational cultures to resolve emerging internal conflict rather than assume that expectations are standard, rely on established environmental trends, or assume agreement as to the lessons of institutional history.

At the same time, the institutional culture must first adapt to meet new challenges in higher education before governance structures can be altered. In working to encourage the evolution of university cultures—and eventually governance arrangements—leaders need to view our institutions in multiple ways: as organized goal-oriented structures, as sociopolitical and economic entities, as human resource–driven enterprises, and as bearers of symbolic meaning, defining and depicting the relationship between the college or university and the community. Institutional culture can itself be a value-adding and value-creating resource, in terms of both the educational experience provided to students and the environment created for faculty and administrators. Some initial steps in making institutional culture a valuable resource may involve encouraging the development of a culture of celebration where collective, rather than only individual, victories are publicly valued and where service to colleagues, the institution, and the community becomes much more than stripes toward the achievement of tenure and promotion or a means of developing and more effectively positioning the institution in the market. Another worthwhile step may be the identification of specific nodes of excellence, or market niches, to be pursued and particular blends of curricular and cocurricular experiences that can make a difference to evaluated and perceived student outcomes—while bearing in mind that strategic planning can be a two-edged sword, as the process itself can stultify and fossilize as well as energize and encourage.

Given that the functions of teaching and learning are central to all universities, governance structures should be continually evaluated from the perspective of their contribution toward the strengthening of a learning culture, and leaders should insist on student-centeredness as essential to the mission of the institution. Constant scrutiny of these functions is vital to the transformation process. Rolling coalitions, constituted from as many groups and individuals as possible, can help to keep the change process moving forward. In forming such coalitions, trustees, administrators, and faculty leaders need to delineate clearly the responsibilities and primary interests of all constituents in the governance process while establishing mechanisms that ensure linkage between accountability and authority. It is extraordinarily difficult to abandon the notion that sharing authority diminishes it, yet shared governance requires open communication and trust predicated on mutual respect, agreed-upon parameters for the decentralization of authority and responsibility, and broad understanding of leadership roles in the institution. Even when these steps are taken, it remains essential to maintain balance through perspective, humor, and a tolerance for ambiguity. After all, an effective governance structure will seem to function slowly compared with the pace at which new challenges inevitably arise.

In the course of encouraging constructive cultural and structural change, no single approach to leadership suffices. Leaders, whether faculty or administrators or trustees, need to deploy multiple frames of reference in the development of a new consensus on governance, simultaneously as well as successively. Leaders who have a clear personal vision are most likely to be effective in working with a range of models of institutional structure. Even when dialogue among trustees and faculty, students, administrators, alumni, parents, community members, and legislators is facilitated in a productive, mutually supportive context, such discussions can sometimes reveal previously unrecognized disparities in attitudes and values. Often, it appears easier to eliminate unnecessary boundaries between trustees, administrators, and faculty in private universities than in public universities, where trustees are typically appointed by state governors and may be regarded, accurately or not, as wedded to a particular political and market agenda. At the same time, we feel it necessary to emphasize that all trustees have a particular responsibility to observe dysfunctional boundaries in their universities and colleges and to work toward transcending them by earning trust, rather than simply by attempting to exercise authority.

This work presents an overview of the literature on the state of university governance, focusing primarily on those issues that bear on higher education leadership and management, technology, teaching and learning, and budgeting. A content analysis of the concepts, issues, and indicators discussed in the literature suggests that they are all central to the higher education enterprise. It also reviews several surveys of faculty leaders and administrators and examines trustees' perspectives so as to better understand their observations and perceptions regarding governance issues. Given the concern of this work with longer-term issues of governance, management, and leadership, surveys of students' attitudes have not been included. Nevertheless, we remain cognizant of the nexus between governance structure and student interests in matters such as access, the quality of teaching and learning, and the availability of related services. One of our objectives is also to recognize patterns among governance models, as well as constraints on and opportunities for reform of governance. Finally, because the effective management of conflict is so vital to the university governance process, we identify and consider sources of continuing conflict in attitudes toward governance, inside and outside the academy.

Even if the traditional concept of governance itself implies hierarchical decision making, the structure and goals of universities will probably remain distinct from those of corporations. Perhaps more effective university governance requires a redefinition and renewed sense of community. This renewal may begin with the concept of confidence building, over time, based on intensive, communication-rich interaction between permeable companies of coequals. Conflicting views can be discussed more productively within, rather than across, networks of collegiality, where it may be possible to fold multiple points of view together while connecting past realities to an increasingly consensual vision of the future.

This reach is not improbable. Several recent research projects have identified areas where faculty, administrative leaders, and trustees may have more in common than meets the eye. The key concerns with regard to governance include resources, participation, access, quality, and accountability. Each group wishes to ensure the quality of higher education. Each seeks affordable tuition prices, diverse and well-prepared student populations, and high-quality research, teaching, and service to university communities, despite somewhat divergent connotations and interpretations. Leaders in each group should be challenged to help create a climate for more open communication, including mutually active listening, while making full use of the resources provided by information technology.

There is much to discuss. In the case of teaching and learning, for instance, there is an increasing awareness that the efforts of individual faculty to encourage deep and relational learning can make a difference when systematic institutional support is available. With regard to accountability, emerging evidence suggests the utility and broad acceptability of agreed-upon, institution-specific key performance indicators, with strategic goals clearly linked to budget allocation decisions. Budgetary decentralization can provide incentives for colleges, schools, and departments to undertake excellent teaching, research, and service. At the same time, it is more and more generally understood that academic quality cannot be addressed only by means of quantitative measurements.

Academic leaders seem to agree on an ideal form of governance, in something of a Platonic sense—one supporting the goals of the institution and facilitated by information technology. These areas of actual or tentative convergence represent potential building blocks on which a promising agenda for dialogue might be developed. For instance, where institutional governance encourages information empowerment accompanied by significantly decentralized but coordinated decision making, shared governance appears to be more acceptable to most academic leaders. And personal leadership rooted in cognitive fluidity and complexity is an especially critical independent variable in this equation. The only real difference between building blocks, or stepping stones and stumbling blocks, remains the way in which we use them.

Returning to the deployment of information technology, several encouraging examples of successful collaborative decision making in universities are identified later. But the implementation of an effective information technology strategy demands the application of new models of leadership and management. In turn, the following sections provide evidence that leaders can gain important advantages when we identify and use, rather than misuse, key elements of our university's or college's culture, such as mission, historical traditions, and modal values. Indeed, institutional culture can be seen as a potential competitive advantage, albeit one that might need to be actualized.

Trends in University Governance

T HE TERM *UNIVERSITY GOVERNANCE* can elicit distinctive responses from different people. The very mention of university governance may raise issues that can cause heated discussion among faculty, administrators, and board members. Differences of perspective among key university stakeholders can be extremely divisive—and sometimes unbridgeable. When thinking about the multiple perceptions that attend essential realities, it may be helpful to recall the Sufi parable of the five blind men who had the opportunity to experience an elephant for the first time. The first man approaches the elephant and encounters one of its legs. "Ah, an elephant is like a tree!" he exclaims. The second, who has felt the trunk, says, "No, an elephant is more like a strong hose." The third, grasping the tail, replies, "Don't be foolish; an elephant is like a rope," while the fourth, playing with an ear, proclaims, "No, more like a fan." And the fifth, leaning against the animal's side, firmly declares, "An elephant is more like a wall." Perception is an issue of individual viewpoint. And often, one's point of view shifts relative to location, or as environmental change occurs.

Of course, it remains the case that to be absolutely certain of something, one must either know everything or nothing about it. With the increase in significance of tertiary education over the last fifty years, perspectives on higher education have also proliferated. Everyone has an opinion based on his or her perspective, and these opinions often disagree. Those who have some knowledge of higher education and its context, however, are all likely to agree that the higher education environment has changed and is continuing to change significantly. This change has forced all those involved in higher education to question traditional approaches and methodologies.

It is therefore not surprising that interest in the topic of higher education governance is extremely high. The reference list ending this volume simply indicates, without any claim to inclusiveness, the currently available range and variety of books and articles concerned with higher education governance. A rapid search of Web-based resources in mid-2002 listed 16,800 Web sites relating to governance in higher education. This evident interest is heightened further by the news that emanates from college and university campuses each day, much of which reflects the changing higher education environment.

Around the world, universities and their governance systems are experiencing change that occurs when accumulating environmental alterations force significant adjustments in the properties of a substance or, in this particular case, institutional identity. For instance, when water is heated to a determinate point, 100 degrees centigrade, it becomes gaseous. When heat energy is applied to water, it changes states from liquid to gas. One might argue that energy, albeit in a different form, is being applied to higher education. Structural and institutional changes have resulted. In 1983, George Keller argued that higher education in the United States, and elsewhere, had entered a revolutionary period in which finances, student numbers, course or program demand, scheduling, educational technology, the nature of the faculty, and expanding external regulation were sharply changing. They are some of the energy sources impelling change in the form, substance, and processes of higher education, including university governance.

Financial concerns may represent the largest single factor. In the United States, inflation-adjusted growth in first federal, then state, funding of higher education has ended, while regulatory and policy pressures have significantly increased. In 1933, for example, states contributed about half of public college and university operating budgets, but this ratio had fallen to 33 percent only a decade later. A study released by the National Association of College and University Business Officers (NACUBO) during its annual conference in August 2001 found that almost every institution was spending more than it charged to educate undergraduates. For instance, public four-year universities reported tuition gaps ranging from $4,000 to $10,000, private counterparts indicated that such gaps averaged $20,000 per student, and community colleges documented differences between tuition payments and expenditures ranging from $3,000 to $7,000. Where private four-year colleges spent an average of 70 percent of their budgets on instruction, community colleges spent 86 percent of their funding on teaching, and public four-year institutions expended 87 percent of their resources on classroom education (National Association of College and University Business Officers, 2001).

In the Caribbean, where higher education has traditionally been funded by national governments and where tuition costs have been a factor only over the last two decades or so, tuition payments account for less than 12 percent of the actual cost of a student's education, while more and more students are demanding access. In the United Kingdom as well, increasingly larger numbers of universities compete for state funds, and student fees constitute only a small percentage of the real cost. Cost pressures and access limitations relative to demand have fueled a debate in the United Kingdom as to whether to impose higher tuition fees or an education tax. In 2003, the Higher Education Funding Council for England began to distribute funding to universities with the goal of encouraging specialization, based on their performance records in teaching and research. Cambridge, Oxford, the University College of London, and Imperial College shared more than 300 million pounds, or over a third of the total research funding available (Goddard, 2003).

In the United States, demand for education has also expanded, as more than 60 percent of all high school graduates continued on to some form of postsecondary education. For instance, a record 15.3 million students enrolled in colleges and universities in the fall 2001 semester. The U.S. Department of Education projected that national enrollment would grow by an additional 16 percent from 2001 to 2011, mainly because of the growing college-age population. During 1990–2000, the value of private university endowments tripled, and higher education became a $260 billion market. Entry barriers remained substantial, given the capital costs required for campus construction. The supply of faculty members exceeded demand, as more doctoral degrees were awarded than the number of available faculty positions.

The growth trend is similar for the Caribbean and Latin America, where playing catch-up, regional governments have set ambitious targets for tertiary expansion, leading to the proliferation of community colleges in the islands of the West Indies as well as the emergence of national universities to complement the University of the West Indies, which has traditionally served the entire region. The University of the West Indies itself is on an expansionist course to meet growing demand, given the articulated goal of Caribbean Common Market countries to increase tertiary-level enrollment from a regional average of 9 percent to 15 percent of the age cohort by 2005. In the United Kingdom, a target of 50 percent has been set as being desirable for participation in some form of postsecondary education, and government agencies are working with various institutions to make it a reality, paradoxically at the very same time that significant increases in university tuition fees are under consideration.

Since 1980, average salaries for U.S. tenure-track faculty rose by 1 percent per year in real terms, while tuition increased at a rate more than three times the consumer price index. A high school diploma became increasingly inadequate for success in the modern economy, and the lifetime earnings of a college graduate were more than twice those of his or her high school counterpart. Consumers had limited leverage over their educational institutions, and because the value of the education provided was mostly ascertainable after the fact, informed decision making was problematic. Customers therefore relied on institutional reputations and rankings to make their choices. One resultant anomaly was that higher tuition costs could actually increase demand when interpreted as a symbol of quality. Meanwhile, competition within state systems was managed so as to prevent facility and course duplication, and among private universities, competition was muted by excess demand. Within the higher education sector, one result was an annual market failure rate (institutional closure or merger) of 1 percent, well below the typical private sector experience of 3 to 5 percent (Collis, 2001).

U.S. and European universities have tended to view the Caribbean as an attractive export market, either through distance education or by joint venture arrangements with local providers at competitive rates. The challenge in the region has been to manage quality assurance in an open market with limited infrastructure. British institutions such as Harriet Watt, Henley-Brunel, Warwick, and Sheffield, the University of New Brunswick (Canada), and American institutions such as the University of Louisiana, Florida International, and Barry University have been quite active in the Caribbean.

During the decade to 1997, 73 percent of all U.S. colleges and universities experienced an increase in the proportion of students requiring remedial education (Levine, 1997). A majority of undergraduates worked while attending college part time. Many state and federal legislators concluded that faculty members cared little about undergraduate education, especially for freshmen and sophomores, preferring instead to focus on research and graduate education (Layzell, 1992). In fact, a radical shift in the nature of demand for higher education was under way. Employers, workers, and students increasingly valued lifetime education following a baccalaureate or, increasingly, a master's degree, given accelerating knowledge accumulation and the adoption of new technologies (Collis, 2001). Various constituents demanded improved accountability and greater relevance from higher education—nothing new to higher education, but their importance was increasing. The need to manage quality assurance effectively in the Caribbean has already been mentioned. It should also be pointed out that with tertiary expansion in the region, the community colleges and newer tertiary institutions have assumed that remedial education will become a fact of life, and some have made provisions for this reality, especially in vital areas such as English and mathematics.

At the same time in the United States, significant numbers of faculty members, particularly in business, computer science, engineering, and the natural sciences, were functioning as academic entrepreneurs, leading research units with millions of dollars of revenues (Etzkowitz and Stevens, 1998). The Bayh-Dole Act of 1980, which allowed universities to patent the results of research funded by the federal government, was an especially important watershed. Before the passage of this legislation, universities were producing approximately 250 patents per year (Press and Washburn, 2000). In contrast, during 1998 alone, universities produced more than 4,800 patent applications. To be sure, it is estimated that only one in ten patented discoveries will earn enough to cover filing costs, while only one in ten thousand will yield substantial returns (Bowie, 1994). Even so, academic entrepreneurs clearly spend more time than ever before applying for external funding and seeking to develop patented products, while institutions commit unprecedented levels of resources and support personnel to manage grants, contracts, technology transfer arrangements, and other related activities. This dual role of colleges and universities as both teaching institutions and research and development centers has caused problems. For instance, a spring 2003 survey of public opinion on higher education found that general undergraduate education, and workforce and teacher training were the highest priorities, whereas state legislators, governors, and university leaders have usually emphasized research related to economic development and corporate competitiveness (Hebel, 2003). Perceptions concerning the definition of institutional role also vary, sometimes dramatically. Who is to manage the tensions between teaching and learning on the one hand, and research and development on the other? And how is accountability to be pursued across an institution that must win resources through the linked talents of a variety of individuals so that its reputation, and therefore organizational viability, might increase?

Faculty members, administrators, and trustees all have their own at least somewhat different perspectives as to who is "in charge" and just why "they" are (Hodgkinson, 1969; McConnell, 1970; Keeton, 1971; Riley and Baldridge, 1977; Howerton, 1996; Leatherman, 1999). The perceived implications of fiduciary responsibility and its locus provide a good example of some of the challenges of governance. *Black's Law Dictionary* defines a fiduciary as "one who owes to another the duties of good faith, trust, confidence and candor." Among higher education leaders, however, this term has been used in varying ways, offensively and defensively. Questions recur as to who actually possesses fiduciary responsibility and why.

The Association of Governing Boards's *Effective Trusteeship* (Ingram, 1995) outlines twelve primary responsibilities, ranging from "setting mission and purposes" to "serving as a court of appeal." None reference fiduciary responsibility, but the author approvingly quotes J. L. Zwigle, who opened the Association's Washington, D.C., office in 1963 and served as president from 1963 to 1973. According to Zwigle, "The trustee has only one basic obligation: to exercise judgment on issues of policy without undue regard for pressures or opinions to the contrary: the trustee must then do whatever is possible as a member of the corporation to see that decisions are in fact carried out" (Ingram, 1995, p. 21). We will explore the interplay between the AGB's perspectives and those of the American Association of University Professors in the next chapter and also review related surveys later.

As a working definition for higher education, fiduciary responsibility may be seen as the legally enforceable duty of trustees, the president, and officers of a university to fully abide by all relevant policies and bylaws as well as applicable federal and state laws, regulations of accrediting professional associations and accreditation commissions, and collective bargaining agreements that the institution has committed to uphold (Payette, 2001).

The avoidance of conflicts of interest is an important element of fiduciary responsibility. Thus, in the 1995 *Adelphi University* case, the New York State Board of Regents took a dramatic step and removed the trustees from office on the grounds of such conflicts as well as neglect of duty, misconduct, and failure to carry out the educational purposes of the university.

The role of the faculty senate in governance provides another good example of perceptions in conflict or at cross purposes. For many faculty members, the senate is an essential means of collective expression, exemplifying the democratic process. More than a few faculty senates, however, are criticized as debating clubs whose active members do not represent the mainstream of faculty thinking (Jordan, 2001). Prominent faculty members may not participate, because there are no rewards. Some professors who engage in academic politics may not be seen as strong teachers and researchers. Senates have often been criticized for focusing on vested interests such as salary, rank, tenure, promotion, and departmental prerogatives (Birnbaum, 1989, 1991).

Yet some faculty senates are known to play a positive role, especially when the majority of their members are effective scholars and teachers concerned about maintaining the university's educational mission (Henderson, 1967; Brown, 1991; Friedman, 1996). Key to a successful faculty-administration relationship is a sense of partnership capable of supporting a culture of shared enthusiasm. As always, however, prescriptions are more easily provided than followed.

The complexities of governance accumulate when we take account of external pressures to which colleges and universities must respond. Higher education drives society only to the extent that it demonstrably meets significant social needs. An important point of contention among higher education leaders is how to respond to societal pressures, specifically to which ones, and how rapidly. Such pressures, including changes in demographics, expectations of participation, technology, and resources, have initiated policy reassessments on the part of many leaders. In certain cases, these pressures have led to reforms or reconsidered and redesigned curricular and pedagogical philosophies, enrollment management practices, student services, budgeting and financial policies, and community relations.

Institutional transformation is a deep and pervasive intentional process, however. It must be preceded and accompanied by alterations in underlying assumptions, behaviors, processes, and outputs (Eckel, Hill, and Green, 1998). Over time, the effective transformation of universities and colleges enhances their abilities to perform their fundamental missions of teaching, research, and service (Astin and Associates, 2001).

In thinking about the extent to which institutional reforms are both fundamental and effective, it is helpful to focus on core mission elements. Thus, unless curricular and cocurricular reforms actually involve significant changes in the processes of teaching and learning, it may be argued that such reforms are epiphenomenal. Wilber (1998) suggests a 2 × 2 evaluative matrix that includes *individual consciousness* (values, beliefs, and expectations), *individual actions* (teaching, research, advising, planning), *institutional structures* (departments, programs, policies), and *institutional culture* (shared values, shared assumptions, and shared beliefs). Institutional transformation, including enduring reforms, takes place in all four quadrants (see Figure 1).

FIGURE 1
Institutional Transformation: Challenges and Opportunities

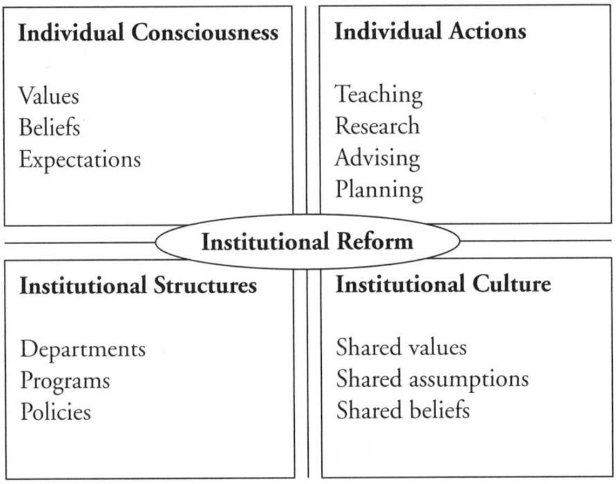

Individual Consciousness	**Individual Actions**
Values Beliefs Expectations	Teaching Research Advising Planning

Institutional Reform

Institutional Structures	**Institutional Culture**
Departments Programs Policies	Shared values Shared assumptions Shared beliefs

Source: Wilber, 1998, p. 71.

Changes in institutional culture tend to occur especially slowly. Because emotional pain is inevitable, efforts at transformation generate resistance. Indeed, there must be some institutional readiness to change if any success is to be achieved at all. Eckel, Hill, Green, and Mallon (1999) speak of calm waters, where there is little perceived need to change; currents; rapids, indicating apparent hazards; and the edge of the waterfall, where a sense of crisis can create consensus about immediate and far-reaching change.

In any case, it is clear that successful institutional transformation involves adjusting some elements of institutional culture and preserving or strengthening others. It is also important to differentiate between defenders of the status quo and constructive skeptics while keeping all stakeholders informed and inviting feedback. Established governance procedures may well be part of what needs changing. A summation of the more effective strategies for institutional transformation includes:

- Generating support from external stakeholders and developing positive publicity for the outcomes expected from the proposals for change
- Maintaining open channels of communication within the campus community
- Relating the explicit or espoused values inherent in the institutional mission statements to the proposed changes, by either contrast or extension
- Collaborating with peer institutions so that experiences, insights, and data can be shared
- Using the strategic planning process as a means of clarifying or even redefining institutional mission and purpose
- Ensuring that newly recruited personnel buy in to articulated institutional change strategies
- Encouraging all members of the campus community to develop a shared understanding of the overall transformation project
- Creating a culture of celebration rather than one of blame assignment and recognizing the contributions of all participants in a timely manner
- Using program review (including outside consultants) and proactive assessment to create a climate for change while also shaping the change process and building support for it

- Encouraging teams of faculty and staff to participate in relevant national or regional professional association meetings.

Given the nature of the higher education environment, the prime competitive goals of institutional transformation frequently cluster around the reputation of specific services or programs and the prestige of the institution as a whole (Goldman, Gates, and Brewer, 2001). Whereas reputation can be measured in absolute terms such as acceptance, retention, and graduation rates, it is ironic that many universities tend to pursue prestige through three totally unrelated "prestige generators": relative quality of incoming students (SAT scores), available federal research funding (dollars), and the success of athletics programs (won-lost records). Success in the pursuit of prestige tends to encourage enhanced private donations and public appropriations, yet it may be achieved at the expense of at least some programs and services. The classic example is that of the large research university where first- and second-year undergraduates are taught mainly by teaching assistants and adjunct professors.

Further, the competition for students with desirable characteristics or the development of expensive research facilities may lead to cross-subsidization, high tuition costs, and inattention to the needs of some stakeholders. Institutional excellence may be seen as an issue of reputation and resources, student and alumni outcomes, or effective educational practices and processes. National magazine rankings focus on reputation, counting things that are countable rather than the things that count. Outcome assessment remains problematic, given wide variances in incoming student characteristics. In fact, if the quality of the educational experience provided to students is a core concern, factors such as the extent and nature of student-faculty interaction and effective program structure are most important (Pascarella, 2001). In the final analysis, the perceptions of institutional leaders drive decisions as to the competitive goals pursued.

Challenges to University Governance Structures

THE STRUCTURE OF UNIVERSITY governance may be visualized as a series of concentric circles. The inner circle includes university presidents, faculty, senior administrators, and trustees. Other circles contain varying arrays of local community members, alumni, students, state legislators, state governors (who often appoint public university trustees), state departments or boards of education, system-level offices, accrediting institutions, the U.S. Department of Education, related congressional committees, funding organizations, and higher education associations (see Figure 2).

Alternatively, following Birnbaum (1988), the core of university governance may be visualized as a set of *overlapping* circles, with faculty, policies related to academic freedom, and research centers or institutes in one circle; senior administrators, budgets, and regulations in another; and department heads in an overlapping segment (see Figure 3). The division is not clear-cut, as faculty and administrators move between the technical and administrative cores. For example, senior administrators may choose to assume limited teaching responsibilities, and faculty committees may have administrative functions. We will further consider Birnbaum's analysis of the structure and dynamics of academic organizations when discussing alternative approaches to institutional structure.

Governance Structures in Historical Perspective

In colonial America, the governing board and college president in practice had exclusive authority over all management and leadership functions (Lucas, 1994). For example, although the College of William and Mary's

FIGURE 2
Visualizing University Governance: Concentric Circles

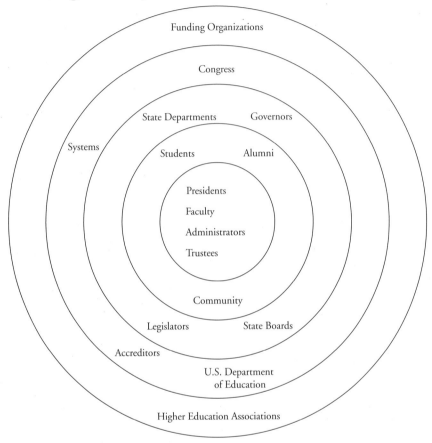

charter gave faculty the authority to appoint presidents and legislate for the college, the trustees did not feel able to include faculty members in decision making until the passage of three decades (Brubacher and Rudy, 1997). Similarly, at Harvard, it was not until 1825 that faculty protests concerning administrative decision making and the nature of the curriculum led to greater faculty influence over the processes of teaching, learning, and student discipline (Wolfe, 1996). University governing boards were traditionally chartered by the state and elected by the state citizenry or appointed by the state governor or legislature. These boards often provided benevolent, nonintrusive

FIGURE 3
Visualizing University Governance: Overlapping Circles

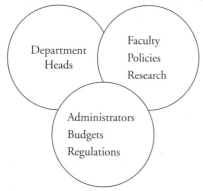

Source: Birnbaum, 1988, p. 55.

oversight while offering political and fundraising support, hiring presidents, and reviewing budgets (Glenny and Dalglish, 1973). Expectations of trustees' institutional stewardship expanded over time but continued to be often regarded as a mainly symbolic act in which trustees approved annual institutional budgets, assured financial viability, decided upon investments in new buildings and equipment, led fundraising efforts, and established guidelines for endowment management.

Higher education institutions can be seen as quintessentially political entities. They control significant public resources and have the authority to allocate costs and benefits selectively (Pusser and Doane, 2001). Politically salient policy contests continually occur within universities, concerning issues such as affirmative action, student conduct codes, faculty promotion and tenure, academic freedom, and resource allocation. Historically, throughout periods of reassessment and reform, questions and doubts are naturally raised about the meaning, the locus, and the reach of authority, responsibility, influence, and accountability on our campuses. Although colleges and universities respond differently in scope and speed to social and market conditions, institutional behavior and evolution depend closely on the process and structure of authoritative decision making, regardless of the setting. It took years, for example, before the Council of Oxford University finally agreed to establish a Business School in the name of its principal benefactor, even though market demand and the need for a change in the traditional Oxford image suggested that it was the reasonable thing to do.

University governance structures have undergone a sea change since the days of relatively independent presidents such as Charles William Eliot of Harvard, Woodrow Wilson at Princeton, and Benjamin Jowett at Balliol College, Oxford, during the late nineteenth century (Kerr and Gade, 1989). Institutional leaders have led and managed reassessment and reforms as a result of cumulative changes in the higher education environment.

Governance, Management, and Leadership

The foundation for effective governance processes rests on a clear understanding of the relationship between the assigned governance roles of faculty leaders, senior administrators, and trustees, regardless of whether these relationships are clear or blurred. To further clarify its meaning, the word *governance* denotes both the structure and process of authoritative decision making across issues that are significant for external as well as internal stakeholders. The related concepts of *management* or *administration* focus on the implementation of decisions, while *leadership* refers to the roles and processes through which individuals seek to influence decision. These latter three concepts are complementary rather than contrasting, however.

Let us consider leadership, therefore, as a critical aspect of governance. Leadership may be initially approached as instrumental, inspirational, informal, or illusionary. Where *instrumental* leadership involves exchange relationships, the *inspirational* leader may be transformational, charismatic, and visionary; an *informal* leader may be elected, emergent, or nonappointed; and an *illusionary* leader can include implicit and romantic approaches to leading, applying noncontingent rewards and punishments (Yammarino and Dansereau, 2001).

Alternatively, leadership may be seen as an issue of personal dominance, interpersonal influence, or relational dialogue. From the perspective of personal dominance, a leader possesses special characteristics that elicit commitment and acceptance among followers. In turn, interpersonal influence occurs when a collegial group argues and disagrees, plans and negotiates, until someone emerges as the single most influential person. Relational dialogue may occur when people working together use dialogue and collaborative learning to accomplish their objectives by embracing differential perspectives, values, and beliefs (Drath, 2001). At least eight images of leadership can be discerned, however, blending anecdote and experience (Lee and King, 2001):

- Genetic leadership—The assumption is that some people are born with leadership talents, others not, and only certain people can learn to lead effectively.
- Learning to lead—One can be an effective leader by studying leadership carefully and practicing what he or she studied.
- Heroic leadership—Good leaders perform courageous, wise, and benevolent feats that others cannot.
- Leading from the top—Leadership occurs only at or close to the top of an organization.
- Social script leadership—When it is the proper time for one to lead, he or she will be asked to do so and should gracefully accept.
- Position leadership—A person with the job and title is a leader, and others will expect him to lead.
- A calling for leadership—This image involves a deeply felt sense of mission, private purpose, and inevitability about the mantle of leadership.
- A personal vision of leadership—This image is based on rational responses to such questions as Who am I? What do I want to become? How will being a leader help me to become the person I want to be? How can I use my organization to fulfill this personal vision?

A leader who has attained a significant level of self-understanding and who is clear about his or her priorities may be called an authentic leader (Ruderman and Rogolsky, 2001). It is difficult to lead when distracted by inner conflict. In general, workers who are authentic bring their whole selves to their jobs and participate fully in the implementation of organizational goals.

Authenticity has five defining characteristics, some interrelated:

- Clarity concerning one's values, priorities, and preferences
- Acceptance of the necessity for choices and trade-offs in life
- A strong sense of self-determination

- Willingness to work toward aligning one's values and behaviors
- High degree of comfort and satisfaction with decisions made earlier in life.

An authentic leader or manager is better able to cope with the inevitable uncertainties of organizational life, whether by tolerating, coping, accepting, or embracing such realities. A strategic approach of this kind allows managers to anticipate and evaluate environmental changes, tailoring responses to the projected opportunities and risks in a deliberate manner (Sevier, 2000). Among the venerable misconceptions of management and leadership are that failure is harmful, that consistency is always important, and that answers are more important than questions. Further, it is not always a bad idea to postpone decision making, although effective leaders should be wary of looking too far ahead. An existing order may inhibit deeper understanding (Clampitt and DeKoch, 2001).

Whereas many people immediately place events or acquaintances in categories such as good or bad, true or false, black or white, or friend or foe, a truly effective leader needs to be able to see the shades of gray inherent in a situation. This ability derives from a willingness to defer judgment until all the relevant facts and circumstances are known or until circumstances force a decision, regardless. Listening in this manner allows the leader to absorb stories, reports, suggestions, and complaints without offering a definite response. It is also important for leaders to reserve for themselves only the most important decisions and to delegate the rest. A related rule might be "Never make a decision today that you can reasonably put off until tomorrow" (Sample, 2001, p. 39).

In the same spirit, progress usually requires decision making based on incomplete information (Hirschorn, 1997). Uncertainty may be an issue of ignorance, apparently random environmental changes, or situational complexity. Esther Barrazone, Chatham College president for more than a decade, came to exemplify leadership based on effective interpersonal influence and an emphasis on rapid decision implementation (in "Chatham time"), given the availability of sufficient information upon which to act. Each type of uncertainty implies the appropriateness of differential but always authentic responses. Leaders and managers tend to be most conscious of the need to be authentic when attending to long-ignored goals or passions, addressing inconsistencies in their lives, suppressing personal style (perhaps to fit with organizational culture), or responding to major life events.

Despite the existence of an extensive literature concerning effective leadership, academic leadership remains a subject partly shrouded in myth. Do the standard conventions of leadership apply to institutions of higher learning? For instance, it is often asserted that constituents want to have confidence that their leaders know where they are going and that academic leaders therefore require a vision. But an accepted vision is not created out of whole cloth, expressing the leader's goals. Rather, such a vision reflects extensive and active listening. Similarly, whereas attempts at transformational leadership often fail and transactional leadership emphasizes the status quo, good leaders actually help to change their institutions by means of transactions that focus on selected values already in place and encourage movement toward related goals. For instance, Patricia Ewers, who retired from the presidency of Pace University in 2000 after almost a decade, recognized the elaborate organization, strength, and traditions of faculty governance at her institution and patiently cultivated a vision of curricular change focused on competitive interdisciplinary programs that would be demanded into the medium-term future. Again, the magnetic personal qualities of the charismatic leader may provide extra influence, encouraging higher levels of institutional performance, but charisma can also be associated with intolerance, a grandiose sense of certainty, and weakened governance structures (Birnbaum, 1992).

Governance structures are increasingly challenged by changes in educational technology, resources, and participation. As an initial step, such challenges may be better understood by identifying shared, differing, divergent, and convergent perspectives of influential individuals in our university communities, particularly those who are able to develop a personal vision of leadership. The next step is to begin implementing such visions in specific institutional structures by aligning vision and agreed priorities with a clear operational plan. A good leader is essential for facilitating the sifting out of contending views, for sharpening focus, and for creating the conditions for such alignment to take place.

Depicting Institutional Structure

Institutional structure is at least as important for governance as the attitudes and values of individual leaders. Several models describe college/university organizational structure. Such structures may be depicted by means of an organizational taxonomy, including bureaucratic, bureaucratic-academic, academic-bureaucratic, and academic universities (Hendrickson and Bartkovich, 1986). In *bureaucratic* institutions, administrators predominate, faculty and departmental autonomy is minimal, and labor relations are adversarial. In *bureaucratic-academic* colleges, however, a faculty senate and college-wide committees make decisions within narrowly defined areas. In turn, in the *academic-bureaucratic* university, an extensive set of academic policies and procedures are in place, monitored by curriculum committees. Finally, in *academic* institutions, curricular decisions, as well as promotion and tenure, are firmly vested with faculty in departments or colleges.

Robert Birnbaum (1988) dissects the structure and dynamics of academic organizations, wielding the analytic tools provided by models of tightly and loosely coupled collegial, bureaucratic, political, anarchical, and cybernetic systems. Each system has implications for effectiveness in leadership styles, management approaches, and organizational functioning. For instance, in *collegial* systems, it is essential for senior administrators to avoid giving orders that will not be obeyed. In *political* systems, in turn, leaders are encouraged to help clarify group values and to reduce participation costs in the interests of inclusiveness. By contrast, in *bureaucratic* systems, decision making is compartmentalized and highly structured, while in *anarchical* organizations, goals are vague and decision-making processes obscure. Finally, in *cybernetic* systems, leaders must balance persistence and flexibility while learning what to remember and what to forget.

Alternatively, de Groof, Neave, and Svec (1998) refer to collegial, managerial, market, social utility, and political models. The *collegial* model has academic authority residing in disciplinary groups, while the *managerial* model has enterprise-based authority accumulating around the functions of institutional coordination and leadership and system-level authority associated with governmental, bureaucratic, and political power. From the perspective of the *market* model, a university produces services that must be aggressively promoted in a highly competitive market. The *social utility* model emphasizes the principle of equity of access to education, and the *political* model directs attention to the importance of continuous negotiation between university leaders and multiple external sources of funding.

In addressing interlocutors of different persuasions, proponents of each approach may be expected to encounter varying degrees of difficulty concerning the nature of university governance. Yet no single approach is sufficient. As Bolman and Deal (1997) argue, it is helpful to distinguish structural, human resource, political, and symbolic approaches, or *frames,* in the course of understanding and leading organizations. The *structural* frame focuses on established goals and objectives, core processes, strategic planning, and organizational rationality. The *human resource* frame assumes that organizations can only function effectively by serving human needs and that it is essential to identify good fits between individuals and organizations. It is a strategic imperative to invest in people within the institution, taking full account of interpersonal dynamics. An alternative approach is *political,* in which organizations are seen as coalitions of individuals and interest groups. Most important decisions involve who gets what, when, and how. Goals and decisions emerge from bargaining and negotiating. Finally, the *symbolic* frame suggests that the ascribed meaning of activities and events is most important. Such accumulated meanings help to define organizational culture while potentially encouraging passion and purpose among an organization's workers.

Disparities in interpreting governance and its efficacy may stem from the very structure of the university, particularly in institutions where the academic nature of their missions is dominant. As such, it may be unavoidable. Here, companies of equals (many sharing similar career paths and traits such as intellectual confidence and verbal aggressiveness) are expected to work toward common goals and endeavor to reach consensual strategies (Cole, 1993). For example, the faculties at some institutions (Antioch, Bennington, and Goddard Colleges, among others) explicitly emphasize participatory democracy in their searches for or evaluations of senior executives. In fall 2001, the University of West Florida and the Florida Agricultural and Mechanical University provided contrary cases. Mismanagement may be defined, at least implicitly in this context, as insufficient consultation with faculty on the part of administrators. But the indicated solution can often generate new problems. The fact is that institutional structures do have implications for culture and that organizational culture necessarily generates expectations about behaviors and processes. When such expectations are violated or unrealistic, problems may be inevitable.

Shared Governance

These problems are worsened by "surface effects": The word *governance* itself implies a hierarchical decision-making structure (Trow, 1997), which sets up communication traps. When faculty members vote "no confidence" in their university presidents and are overruled by their board of trustees, the sense of such a hierarchy is reaffirmed, whatever the merits of the case immediately in question. This situation is exemplified by the no confidence vote at Goddard College in 1999, in the context of campus community communication difficulties that had persisted at least since 1996. Similarly, controversy could not but attend the reported demand of a University of Toledo board chair in spring 2000 that a group of faculty be immediately terminated, quite apart from the substance of the charges made against them. Again, despite the strong support provided to University of Southern Mississippi President Horace Fleming by faculty and staff members, students, many alumni, and the university's foundation, the state's Higher Education Board extended his contract for only one year in August 2001, citing his "management style" as the reason for their eleven-to-one decision (Basinger, 2001). Questions have emerged and persisted as to whether shared university governance should be revived or eliminated (Leatherman, 1998b).

The concept of shared university governance remains under attack, and it is often blamed for the academy's slow response to change (Hodgkinson and Meeth, 1971). It is worth emphasizing that the operational word here is *shared;* the questions are to what extent and by whom. As for the answers, there seems to be no universal agreement.

As Peterson and Mets (1987) imply, the words *governance, management,* and *leadership* all connote a sense of institutional purpose, direction, and control. Bennis and Nanus (1985) observe that management is about doing things right, while leadership is about doing the right things. Whereas managers administer, maintain, control, and imitate, leaders innovate, develop, inspire, and originate. Managers may adopt a short-term perspective, asking how and when, tending to accept the status quo. Leaders, however, take a long-term view, asking what and why, challenging the accepted order. In turn, "shared governance" can be defined as a mutual recognition of the interdependence and mutual responsibilities among trustees, administration, staff, faculty, and students for major institutional decision making relating to mission, budget, teaching, and research. In principle, full application of this concept can slow the rate of change or even the normal rate of progress in any organization.

Indeed, the situation of slow or no response to changing external conditions on the part of many universities and colleges has been called *paradigm paralysis* (Hooker, 1997). Like members of other human institutions, university community members often find it difficult to adjust the way they think and behave, even when the need for such adjustment is broadly agreed to in principle. As John Dewey (1916) once commented, however, universities and colleges cannot but reflect the society within which higher education is pursued and provided.

As with law, medicine, and the ministry, the academic professoriat has traditionally pursued learning through formalized education and extensive training while exhibiting commitment to a distinctive ideal of public service underpinned by self-regulation in the form of peer review. Relationships between such professionals and the persons served have been explicitly transformational, based on interactions between the parties that are not simply transactional. Within the academy, the practice of shared governance has been held to be a corollary of the concepts of academic freedom and peer review (Hamilton, 2000). It is argued that such shared governance requires the voting faculty to have primary authority over policies for admitting students, the curriculum, procedures for student instruction, standards of student and faculty competence and ethical conduct, and maintenance of the learning environment (Kavanagh, 2000).

As previously noted, higher education arrived at another turning point during the later 1990s when the public (legislators, community leaders, students, parents, and other stakeholders) initiated increasingly critical scrutiny of funding policies, admission practices, and even the curricula and missions of colleges and universities. The forces of change began to influence the mature and competitive industry represented by higher education. Like their corporate counterparts, higher education leaders realized that they were certainly not immune to fundamental environmental pressures and could not ignore at least implicit attacks, whether inherently justified or not.

Appropriate responses are still being articulated or contemplated. Some of the envisaged changes may even touch upon widely adopted, and deeply ingrained, organizational structures. Here a major paradox emerges: How seriously can an organization pursue change if decisions about its future and structure involve rethinking its fundamental reason for being as well as many of the vital interests of its significant constituencies? If it is true that on most campuses, decision-making processes suffer from a diffusion of authority, lack of accountability, limited information, and dysfunctional time frames (Miller, 1998), then the implied projection and acceptance of such negative mirror images of governance may be among the most rooted obstacles to institutional change.

AAUP Versus AGB Perceptions

It is worth reiterating that the very concept of university governance and how the term is defined depend on where you stand. Without positing false dichotomies, trustees, faculty members, and senior administrators tend to have different goals and objectives (Carnegie Commission, 1973). These differences influence how they use and define *governance,* especially when the adjective *shared* is added. Such variances are perhaps clearest when we compare the American Association of University Professors (AAUP) *Statement on Government of Colleges and Universities* (1968) with the Association of Governing Boards of Universities and Colleges (AGB) *Statement on Institutional Governance* (1999).

In 1966, the AAUP and the AGB, along with the American Council on Education (ACE), jointly proposed a statement on university governance. The AGB commended the statement to its members but did not endorse it.

The statement was an attempt to define what has come to be known as "shared governance." The original language tried to establish a mutual understanding as to how college and university governance should operate. It recognized the interdependence of trustees, faculty, and administrators.

After more than thirty years, the Association of Governing Boards in 1998 adopted its own statement on institutional governance. The new statement was clearly directed toward the governing boards' viewpoint that "ultimate responsibility for the institution rests in its governing board" (Association of Governing Boards, 1998, p. 5). The difference between the viewpoints of AAUP and AGB quickly erupted into printed debate. Two important and relevant opinion essays appeared in *The Chronicle of Higher Education* during 1999. The first, written by the president of AAUP, James T. Richardson, was published in February 1999. Cary Nelson authored the second, "The War Against the Faculty," in April 1999. Both writers perceived the AGB statement as further erosion of faculty influence in the decision-making process in higher education.

An opinion article in *The Chronicle of Higher Education* by Richard T. Ingram (1999), then president of AGB, followed these essays in May. In his article, Ingram attempted to encourage discussion between the sides. He called for open and honest debate while reaffirming the AGB's position that the board of trustees was the responsible authority in governing institutions of higher learning. The debate has continued, with publication in *Academe* of "Inextricably Linked," which points out that AAUP has "closely connected, arguably inextricably linked" the relationship of academic freedom with shared governance (Gerber, 2001, p. 1).

Curricular matters continue to present the single most important flashpoint for perceptions of shared governance. For example, the AGB comments that a board has a particular obligation to understand its institution's academic activities, to be certain that these activities support the mission, and to be comfortable with the norms and culture underlying them (Frances, Huxel, Meyerson, and Park, 1987). The authors comment that trustees should generally avoid examining how each course is taught while approving what is taught in terms of major instructional program offerings, as major new program developments usually have implications for institutional mission and finances. The perceived lines between the *how* and the *what* of courses taught are not necessarily always clear, however, and insufficient trust in an institution can only exacerbate the possibility of dissension between faculty, administrators, and trustees.

From the perspective of faculty, the erosion of academic freedom often drives such dissension. Yet O'Neil (2001) contends that academic freedom is actually a most elusive concept. A student would stress the liberty to choose courses (and withdraw from or drop them), select topics for papers, raise questions in class, and post material on the Internet. A professor might emphasize the right to speak and write freely without reprisal (whether as a scholar or as a citizen), to pursue controversial research topics, and to shape course content. In turn, an administrator could stress institutional autonomy. The AGB has argued that trustees should be able to articulate the value of academic freedom and to defend it on behalf of their institutions and individual professors (Ingram, 1996). But observers such as O'Neil are clear that the sanctity of academic freedom does not preclude appropriate oversight, on the part of trustees, over academic policy. The question of what is appropriate remains at issue. The basis for an answer may be found in consensual limits on academic freedom. Even a long-tenured professor can be dismissed for refusal to teach assigned courses or a demonstrated lack of competence in his own discipline or fiscal exigency or medical evidence indicating lack of fitness to fulfill the terms and conditions of appointment.

In 1995, Richard Chait accurately projected that university trustees would become more involved in dialogue with faculty, students, administrators, alumni, parents, community members, and legislators concerning educational issues. Indeed, trustees have been increasingly likely to insist that topics once considered off limits be open for examination. Examples include promotion and tenure decisions, the academic quality of particular departments, faculty workloads, and the application of admissions criteria. From the perspectives of many faculty as well as administrators, shared governance has sometimes degenerated into intrusive trustee governance. But it remains possible to turn such scenarios of potential if not actual culture clash into collaboration by active listening, clearly communicated priorities, strategically delayed judgment, and a cultivated tolerance for ambiguity (Gayle, Hakim, Agarwal, and Alfonso, 1999).

A universally accepted approach to university governance is unlikely to be achieved. Yet governance remains an issue of the locus and reach of power and influence—of how this power should be balanced, distributed, and checked. Universities and other higher education institutions are likely to come under more rather than less scrutiny over the years ahead as the arguments linking the quality and relevance of education to the nature of intellectual capital input into the political economy, and the extent to which it impacts a society's social and economic progress, become more prominent. Thus, the need for oversight of strategic direction and for performance evaluation will probably intensify, even as a stakeholder approach to university governance continues to evolve. The pertinent questions for consideration are What are the ways in which these processes will likely impact self-regulation, and to what extent is the relative autonomy of higher education institutions apt to be eroded?

Accountability and Program Review

Another challenge to governance is consequently an increasing emphasis on accountability, program review, and performance funding or budgeting at many universities. Accountability denotes a process of providing broad quantitative information to oversight bodies, usually including state legislatures, on measures such as net expenditure per full-time enrolled student, the number of lower-division classes taught by adjunct professors, or student retention and graduation rates. Other popular performance funding indicators include time to degree, noninstructional costs in proportion to all costs, program duplication across campuses, alumni and employer satisfaction, sponsored research funds obtained, institutional involvement in teacher education, student test scores, endowment size, fundraising results, job placements after graduation, average salary in year following graduation, and workforce training and development.

By 1997, thirty-seven states reported use of such performance-based measures in the course of policymaking, and eight states engaged in performance funding, which links institutional process measures of this kind to part of its allocation (Callan, Doyle and Finney, 2001). Percentages ranged from less than 1 percent in a number of cases to some 4 percent in Tennessee; in

South Carolina, legislators mandated that 37 performance measures drive the entire state allocation to higher education (Schmidt, 1999). The continuing trend toward performance funding can also be observed in the United Kingdom, Australia, New Zealand, and other countries.

Meanwhile, performance budgeting, which links institutional outputs to dollar allocations using qualitative judgments, was also popular (Burke and Serban, 1998). Processes and outputs are quite distinct from outcomes, however; the full impact of a student's engagement in the learning-teaching process, at any given university, can often be difficult to discern for many years after graduation. A similar comment applies to the commitment of a faculty member to a long-term program of applied or, even more so, basic research. In addition, state accountability measures tend to reward outputs or narrowly defined outcomes such as graduation rates without considering input differences such as students' preparation for university (Layzell and Lyddon, 1990).

More recent process indicators include the proportion of faculty applying information technology to their courses and assessments of student learning beyond the classroom (Gentemann, Fletcher, and Potter, 1994). Such process indicators may be seen as provisional proxies for outcomes, which are usually difficult to measure accurately (Wohlstetter and Van Kirk, 1995). They may also be considered as a means of evaluating institutional progress toward best practices. Most process indicators, however, are oriented toward efficiency, in a rather bureaucratic sense, rather than effectiveness. Few address measures of quality, equity, and choice. In 1996, only Tennessee and Missouri included measures intended to address academic excellence in terms of available resources and the scholarly standing of the faculty (Burke, 1997).

The tendency of accountability processes to count the things that are countable rather than necessarily the things that count can leave faculty with the sense that academic decision making is often cast aside in favor of top-down managerial practices. When administrative planning drives decision making about which programs are expendable, how teaching is carried out, and the allocation of resources between teaching and research, the role of the faculty can be marginalized (Carnegie Foundation, 1982; Marcus, 1999).

In response to this threat, Zumeta (1998) proposed six principles for twenty-first-century accountability:

- Academic freedom should be maintained in teaching, research, and scholarship.
- Policymakers should focus on outcomes, leaving institutions to control inputs and processes.
- Accountability efforts should be guided by the premise that some important elements of higher education practice cannot be measured reliably.
- Budgeting should not be so performance driven as to cause fiscal instability from one year to the next.
- Higher priority should be ascribed to academic quality than to cost containment and efficiency.
- Education policymakers and members of the academy should support rather than undermine lay "boundary groups" such as trustees and state-level higher education boards.

But a public perception of rapidly increasing tuition costs tends to swing the policy pendulum farther in the direction of accountability and away from the tradition of academic autonomy and engagement. For instance, General Accounting Office statistics indicate that where the average tuition for a full-time undergraduate student rose by 44 percent during 1990 to 1996, the consumer price index rose by 15.4 percent and the median household income by 13.8 percent during the same period. In turn, from 1977 to 1997, the median family income increased by 10 percent, adjusted for inflation, whereas the real average cost of college attendance rose by 49 percent (National Center for Education Statistics, 1997; U.S. Census Bureau, 1998).

To be sure, the College Board's 1999–2000 annual tuition and student aid report documents that tuition and fees at four-year private colleges had increased by only 4.6 percent, the lowest such rate in many years. But many observers continue to argue that colleges and universities have yet to do everything possible to maximize value for money in education. This approach may focus attention on issues of affordability and financial efficiency rather than quality. In such a context, administrators and trustees may be tempted to consider more than a quite limited role for faculty in university governance as, at best, an unaffordable luxury or an unattainable ideal. The relationship between the cost of education, the value of the education being delivered, and the financing of education continues to spark debate around the globe. The resolution or management of these issues necessarily impacts university governance.

Faculty participation, however, remains essential for successful systems of accountability and program review. Program reviews complement or include typical evaluation processes such as accreditation or reaccreditation, performance-based budgeting, and student outcomes assessment by demonstrating that program quality is systematically and routinely evaluated. The process establishes that resources are expended effectively in support of the mission and goals of each college and department. The results of this assessment influence future planning, including resource allocation (Wergin and McMillan, 1998).

A successful program review system would regularize the evaluation of institutional effectiveness, encourage continuous improvement, facilitate accreditation or reaccreditation, and ensure the generation of meaningful annual planning and accountability reports. It would achieve this result by presenting the review process as an opportunity for greater effectiveness rather than a threat, with faculty leaders involved in defining the critical evaluation questions, sources of evidence, and interpretation procedures. In contrast, faculty will doubtless view an unsuccessful program review system as ritualistic, time-consuming, and mandated from above, with few, if any, real consequences for their professional lives and departments (Wergin and McMillan, 1998).

Barak and Sweeney (1995) report on a national study of some 150 public and private baccalaureate institutions, with the goal of examining the use of program review in institutional planning, budgeting, and student outcomes assessment. In 19 percent of all reported cases, program reviews were either unused or used ineffectively. At a larger percentage of institutions, 30 percent, the linkage between program review and budgeting was either absent or quite unsatisfactory. Similar reactions were received from 42 percent of the respondents in the case of student outcomes assessment.

Barak and Sweeney found that several factors contribute to successful program review:

- Interest and leadership by chairs, deans, and vice presidents
- A decision-making process that fits the institutional environment
- Simple and readily understandable structures and policies
- Attention to each element of the decision-making process
- Realism about exactly what program review can contribute to institutional improvement and the manner in which it functions.

State legislators nevertheless have increasingly demanded standardized program reviews and accountability reports from state universities. During the 1990s, an increasing number of states linked budget appropriations to specific performance measures. Meanwhile, eleven states reorganized the entire process of higher education governance, mainly as a result of political and cultural factors (Coble, 2000). In forty-three states, the governor appointed members of the central higher education board while often also appointing local boards. Program review and accountability processes that effectively address issues of academic quality continued to coexist with processes that tended to focus on readily understood if simplistic standardized performance measures.

An alternate approach to accountability is provided by the use of institution-specific "key performance indicators" linking strategic goals to budget allocation decisions (Dolence and Norris, 1994). For example, the University of Northern Colorado established a set of such indicators tied to five-year and ten-year institutional goals that included the six-year graduation rate, fall-to-fall undergraduate student retention rates, doctoral degrees awarded, student enrollment, and alumni attitude surveys. In the case of Benedictine College, the performance indicator set included deferred maintenance, quality of facilities and campus life, tuition discounting, endowment level, and class size (Honan, 1995). Such an approach identifies clear criteria for measurement and assessment but acknowledges the need for significant institutional autonomy.

Indicators such as those mentioned above are often used in the process of benchmarking: the selection of a group of peer or aspirational institutions on the basis of specific characteristics. Benchmarking is rooted in processes of

Continuous Quality Improvement and Total Quality Management, which have migrated from corporate to academic institutions. There are four primary kinds of benchmarking: internal, competitive, functional, and generic, or "best-in-class." The type of benchmarking that might be most appropriate for a given institution depends upon the processes analyzed, and the data as well as the expertise available. In our view, it remains essential for benchmarked performance indicators to be tailored to the mission, goals, and identity of each university and to be used as interpretive tools rather than ends in themselves.

Structural and Cultural Elements of Governance

UNDERSTANDING THE STRUCTURAL and cultural elements of governance is both essential for successful institutional transformation and particularly challenging, because these elements often appear amorphous as well as inherently intractable.

Organizational Culture

Organizational culture is key to the process and structure of authoritative decision making in universities. In turn, the central beliefs and values that shape an organization's culture and position it in the world are critically affected by the degree of trust evident among participants. Such trust has to be established by the leadership. Sinfonis and Goldberg (1996) present the analogy of a broccoli floret: the pattern is replicated in the cluster of florets that make up the stalk and the stalks that make up the head. Organizational culture can contribute to effective governance only when trust becomes a fractal, part of each participant's basic belief system.

Within organizations, including universities, culture defines appropriate behavior, bonding and motivating individuals, while governing the way in which institutions process information, shaping their internal relations and even values. Such values denote consensual sets of beliefs concerning preferred modes of conduct and desirable objectives (Rokeach, 1973). Alternatively, culture may be viewed as both the framework that influences, and is influenced by, decision making and by the behavior of people making these decisions. Where cultural collegiality is strong, faculty members do not need senates to protect their rights and customs (Bess, 1992). In such cases, organizational culture can lend legitimacy to the process of choosing when difficult choices must be made (Cole, 1993).

To be effective, leaders require contextual intelligence rooted in an understanding of the customs and traditions, historical and philosophical evolution, formal and informal political structures, the language, and the myths that mold a particular organization (Terenzini, 1993). Such intelligence includes an understanding of the assumptions, values, norms, and tangible signs (artifacts) of faculty members, staff, and administrators and their interacting behaviors. The beliefs and practices of trustees, senior administrators, and faculty members regarding the rights and responsibilities of campus community members, competitors, and society are fundamental in shaping organizational culture.

An enduring set of tenets and norms form the basis of the academic social system, generating a shared mental model that allows faculty to attribute merit and meaning to the external and internal events experienced. This model is taken for granted in the absence of significant cognitive dissonance. A consensual learning process results, frequently communicated by individuals and groups verbally and occasionally codified into faculty bylaws and handbooks. Indeed, organizational culture can encourage the construction of widely shared belief systems based on the logic of transference, card stacking, and bandwagon behavior.

In the case of transference, the more often a particular campus community member has been proved to be correct, the more likely, it is felt, he or she will be right in the future. Similarly, card-stacking logic implies that a belief must be true because all the available evidence seen so far supports it, whereas bandwagon reasoning accepts that the more widespread a conviction appears to be among members of a community or organization, the more unassailable it has become (Gilmore, 1997). The relative strength of an organization's culture depends on how well the group deals with recurring needs for external adaptation and internal integration (Millett, 1962; Kochan and Useem, 1992).

Cultures manifest themselves in formal reward systems, socialization mechanisms, and decision-making processes as well as implicit behavioral norms, role models, rituals, organizational language, and history (Victor and Cullen,

1988; Trevino, 1990). Indeed, the independent variables that drive institutional performance include the internal processes by which a university continually renews its knowledge and spirit.

It may be argued that a functional organizational mission exists only when strategy and culture are mutually supportive. Even so, fundamental tensions between organizational strategy and culture are probable, especially in an age of discontinuous change (Handy, 1989). From the perspective of governance, in the longer term the most successful campus cultures appear to those that promote cooperation while encouraging individual achievement. By contrast, cultural norms that emphasize competition instead of internal cooperation tend to encourage dysfunctional behavior, implicitly if not explicitly (Braithwaite, 1989; Baucus and Near, 1991). Additionally, dissonance between the culture of a college campus and the actions of its faculty, administrators, or trustees can result in alienation, gridlock, and crisis (Schein, 1992; Splete and Dickeson, 2001).

Trustees' Perspectives

From the perspective of trustees, the academy is replete with boundaries, especially between trustees and faculty but also between administrators, faculty, students, alumni, and sometimes the external community. These boundaries create significant obstacles to effective governance and can be especially perceptible at independent universities, where trustees may be appointed by state governors rather than selected by the existing board, as with private universities. A faculty member at a research university who had first served as a consultant, then later as a trustee to a liberal arts college, once quipped to the college's academic officers. . . ., "When I was your consultant, you told me everything I needed to know about the college, and paid me, to boot. Now that I am a trustee, you tell me as little as possible, and expect me to pay you!" (Zemsky, Shannon, and Shapiro, 2001, p. 25). Trustees must perceive such boundaries and commit themselves to the dedicated work required to transcend them, despite the authority available to boards of trustees (Chait, 2000).

Effective boards share governance, seeking to create a culture characterized by trust, competence, coordination, and communication (Wilson, 2001). The inherent challenges include the institutionalization of cross-boundary communication so as to maximize thoughtful analysis. Although trustees should view the faculty as the principal resource for informed oversight of academic policies and programs, faculty should recognize the board's responsibility to govern and welcome responsible strategic oversight of the faculty's prerogatives. Meanwhile, the president should bridge the gaps between campus constituencies and the board by coordinating the legitimate strategic interests of faculty, other administrators, and students, then accurately communicating these concerns to the board.

Some observers contrast the *academic* culture, which values freedom of inquiry, intellectual experimentation, tolerance of unconventionality, direct interaction between learners and teachers, pure as well as applied research, and shared governance, with both the *corporate* and the *political* culture. For instance, Bowen (2001) argues that universities began to turn into corporations as a result of the boom economy of the 1990s and the collapse of the Soviet Union. As a result, success was increasingly measured by net income and levels of productivity as market allocations were seen as unquestionable. University presidents became chief executive officers, and provosts became chief operating officers. At the same time, faculty members were transformed into labor and students into customers. Similarly, Brown University's Futures Project reported that consequent to the market inroads made by for-profit higher education providers, more and more college leaders are focusing increasing attention on profitable programs in the interests of institutional survival (Schmidt, 2002). The report concluded that market pressures were endangering the commitment of state universities to their public missions.

The case of a former medical student at Nova Southeastern University depicts one of the potential dangers of an essentially commercial approach to higher education. Nine years after the student sued in 1993 upon receiving a failing grade in the final course required to graduate, the Florida Supreme Court accepted a state appeals court ruling that the university was in breach of contract. The court also accepted the plaintiff's request for damages in the form of the loss of earning capacity that would reasonably have resulted from the receipt of his degree (Makar, 2002). Meanwhile, the political culture was more and more often found among some members of university boards of trustees who took office with the intention of changing academic values to reflect the politics of the elected officials who appointed them, if not to remake the university into a corporation.

Indeed, educational economists have long defined academic efficiency as the use of the minimum necessary resources for intended, rather than actual, results (Halstead, 1989; Thomas, 1998). A focus on the efficiency of universities is by no means recent: during 1894 to 1928, many institutions of higher education adopted faculty recruitment and evaluation systems, financial systems, and accounting standards that approximated those of contemporaneous corporations (Barrow, 1990). For instance, the General Education Board founded in 1903 by John D. Rockefeller endowed colleges and universities across the United States with efficiency as a core concern (Buttrick, 1922).

In 1905, Henry Pritchett, president of the Carnegie Foundation, observed that American universities were tending more and more to conform to the methods of the business corporation in their administration, with a board of directors, a president, subordinate officers, and functionally specialized departments (Pritchett, 1905). Further, one of the first surveys of opinion among university boards of trustees found that the corporate executives who were increasingly in the majority felt that the doctrine of "employment at will" should be applied by boards to university professors (Will, 1901). There truly is nothing new under the sun. Returning to the twenty-first century, if students in many countries around the world continue to seek credentials from prestigious public universities, those looking for employment overseas or with international corporations often prefer to enroll in an independent institution. As Appendix A indicates, where Australia and Sri Lanka have only public universities, 31.1 percent of all U.S. students, 73.9 percent of all Japanese students, and 75.2 percent of all Philippine students enrolled at private universities in 1998.

Organizational Culture and Governance

To recapitulate, perhaps the single most important factor to influence institutional governance is the organizational culture that exists at any given university or college. A strong internal interaction effect exists between organizational culture and governance. It is quite challenging to disentangle the factors that have contributed to the creation of any organizational culture over the decades, such as the impact of particular leaders who have placed their stamp on an institution and the cumulative results of faculty decisions that might come to achieve the status of givens. In turn, the concept of shared governance leaves a great deal of room for individual interpretation. Nevertheless, some evidence exists that a majority of faculty leaders and vice presidents for academic affairs across all institutional categories view organizational culture as both a catalyst for, and a constraint on, shared governance.

Organizational culture can denote the system of shared meaning held by members that distinguishes the organization from all other such groups. College fraternity and sorority organizations are good examples: they include dominant components, with associated strong and weak subcultures, that differentially influence behavior during periods such as rush. Some of the primary dimensions attributed to an organization's culture include a propensity for innovation and risk taking, attention to detail, outcome orientation, people orientation, team orientation, aggressiveness, and stability. One example is Chatham College's reputation for rapid implementation of decisions. These dimensions can be observed in a wide variety of institutions, including clubs, baseball teams, military divisions, and universities.

Another way to think of organizational culture is as the *personality* of an organization, especially colleges and universities. How often have we heard a student talk about how he or she "felt" on campus during an initial visit? Students and faculty soon come to sense the culture of a given college or university. Culture remains a concept in search of decisively consensual transdisciplinary meaning, but most observers of an organization can clearly identify it. One can tell a great deal about the culture of an organization by observing the image projected by major buildings, the extent to which they are maintained, and the arrangements of offices and furniture in them, and by considering what community members brag about and what members wear—just as it is possible to develop a sense of an individual's personality from looking at and listening to him or her.

University leaders increasingly have recognized that the concept of culture is particularly important when attempting to manage university-wide change.

Organizational change must include not only structures and processes but also prior cultural change. Bennis, Spreitzer, and Cummings comment that they had initially approached change management as a matter of combining environmental nudges with the development of organizational scanning, trust, and collaboration (2001). As they later discovered, however, one has to adhere simultaneously to the symbols of tradition and stability and revision and change to be an effective change agent. It is also naturally important for change leadership to be an absorbing passion. W. H. Auden's poetry (1965) captures this thought well:

> *You need not see what someone is doing*
> *To know if it is his vocation,*
> *You have only to watch his eyes;*
> *A cook mixing a sauce, a surgeon*
> *Making a primary incision,*
> *A clerk completing a bill of lading*
> *Wear the same rapt expression,*
> *Forgetting themselves in a function.*

The subject of organizational culture has generated an extensive literature during the past decade, particularly in regard to learning how to effect cultural change. Efforts at organizational change fail on many occasions. Such failure can often be attributed to insufficient understanding of the critical role of culture within organizations, including real and perceived rewards and disincentives, formal as well as informal role distributions, and the philosophy and style of senior managers. This is one of the reasons why many strategic planners now place as much emphasis on identifying core institutional values as they do on mission and vision.

A complex set of forces come together to reinforce the culture and values of an organization. They may include stories told and retold, which take on a mythological character, as well as famous or notorious personalities and dominant individuals who may have had more than their share of influence in shaping the organization's sense of self and its character (Deal and Kennedy, 1982).

Take the case of Robert Hutchins, one of the great presidents of the University of Chicago several decades ago, and his concept of a "learning society," which has greatly influenced the self-perception and external perceptions of the University of Chicago as a community of scholars. Within the framework of this scholarly community, "schools" rather than structured institutions have developed in particular disciplines, denoting frameworks for specific theoretical or conceptual approaches—for instance, the Chicago School of Economics, which acknowledges Frank Knight as the founder and has to its credit an abundance of Nobel Prize winners, and the Chicago School of Literary Criticism, which has a number of distinguished literary scholars associated with it, including Norman McLean, who wrote *A River Runs Through It* long after retirement. Chicago's culture and environment also led to the creation of innovative interdisciplinary institutions not limited to departments or faculties, which enjoy a great deal of autonomy, such as the Committee for Social Thought, once chaired by Nobel Prize–winning novelist Saul Bellow.

Clearly, then, the link between the accepted approach to governance and the culture of a college or university is significant. Whether "administration" serves academic leadership and creativity or determines the direction for academic focus depends largely on the culture of the organization and the evolutionary process that led to the arrival of the institution at a given point in the first place.

Competing Perspectives and Expectations

STAKEHOLDER PERSPECTIVES and expectations about university missions and goals, as well as governance arrangements, sometimes differ significantly. The most challenging differences to address are those involving faculty, senior administrators, and trustees.

Expectations of Faculty, Administrators, and Trustees

Disagreements concerning the meaning and application of governance continue to be pervasive as the twenty-first century gathers pace. Such a clash of perspectives was dramatically illustrated in mid-1998, when the board of trustees at the University of Dubuque requested the Iowa District Court to declare the faculty handbook merely a policy statement, subject to the trustees' approval, rather than a binding contract (*Chronicle of Higher Education,* June 19, 1998, p. A12). In turn, the faculty pointed to several judicial decisions that appeared to establish published and broadly disseminated faculty handbooks as binding contracts.

To recapitulate: on the one hand, the AAUP typically argues that the faculty's voice should be indirectly, if not directly, authoritative across the entire range of university decision making. It is so argued because of the centrality of teaching and research to the academy and the necessary link between such authority and academic freedom (*Academe,* November/December 1994; AAHE-NEA, 1967). On the other hand, governing boards maintain that fiduciary responsibility drives ultimate decision making. For such boards, viable academic governance cannot be isolated from financial exigencies and external conditions such as demographic and cost dynamics (Pew Higher Education Roundtable, 1995). It is held that the role of faculty members is to manage the learning process rather than the institutional learning environment, which is the province of the university administrator, the president, and trustees (Millett, 1980).

Faculty members often argue that university and corporate governance must be differentiated for legal, educational, and social reasons (Cox, 2000). In this view, faculty members participate in management, as asserted by the 1980 *Yeshiva* case, to advance the discovery and dissemination of knowledge, to mold the intellects of their students, and to contribute toward decision making as to the future of the professoriat (Committee T, 1964; AAUP, 1994; Miller, 1996; Armstrong, 2000).

If the Supreme Court held that Yeshiva University's full-time faculty were managers, with the responsibility to develop and enforce employer policies, the members of the majority also indicated that there might be some institutions of higher learning where the faculty was entirely or predominantly nonmanagerial (Baez and Centra, 1995). In independent universities, faculty unionization all but ceased when the Supreme Court then decided that faculty members who participated meaningfully in university management were not eligible to unionize, because they were not simply employees in the usual sense of the term (*National Labor Relations Board* v. *Yeshiva University*, 1980). As a point of comparison, in other countries of the world, notably in Latin America and the Caribbean, faculty members are often unionized and neither lose nor reject their union affiliation upon assuming administrative or managerial responsibilities, including deanships.

Twenty years later, the accepted implications of the *Yeshiva* case began to be called into question, when a National Labor Relations Board (NLRB) regional director found that professors at Manhattan College were not managerial employees, as defined in that case, and therefore could unionize (Leatherman, 2000). This ruling followed a similar one by the full NLRB in the case of the University of Great Falls in Montana, that faculty had an advisory rather than a decision-making role in academic matters.

From faculty's perspective, an ideal governance process includes academic staff at an early stage and empowers faculty to question policy decisions through well-articulated processes (Miller, McCormack, Maddox, and Seagren, 1996). University management structures should be as flat as possible, and administrative decisions should be informed by faculty advice as a matter of course (Michaelson, 1998; Richardson, 1999b; Brown, 2001). Academics are most directly accountable to their professional peers. The core of faculty governance is eviscerated by boards of trustees and administrations that have implemented measures such as posttenure review and shifted resources from low- to high-priority programs despite concerted faculty opposition (Richardson and Rickman, 1998).

For some, this concern was exemplified by Florida International University's closure of its Biomedical Technology Department in 1999, when disagreement between the senior administration and the faculty senate was taken to the state university system's board of regents for resolution. In a particularly ironic example of faculty-administrator conflict, the faculty senate at the University of Notre Dame voted to dissolve itself in May 2001, frustrated by its perceived lack of power or influence, then found that it could not eliminate itself without the approval of the university's academic council, president, and board of trustees (Kellogg, 2001).

Administrators' and trustees' attitudes sometimes stand in stark contrast to those of their faculty counterparts. First, it is commonly asserted that shared governance cannot succeed if faculty members are not ready to think beyond the interests of their own discipline or department in favor of the best interests of their universities as a whole (Keeton and Associates, 1971; Gerber, 1997). Questions are constantly raised about who *decides* as opposed to who *recommends* (Hodgkinson, 1971; Baldridge, Curtis, Ecker, and Riley, 1986; Hollander, 1994). Subtle differences may also exist between faculty members', administrators', and trustees' interpretations of *responsibility* and *authority*. Such issues were at the core of the *Yeshiva* ruling, where Justice Lewis Powell wrote for the majority: "When one considers the function of a university, it is difficult to imagine decisions more managerial than the determination of courses, schedules, tuition, and standards for admission and matriculation."

It was this litmus test that led the NLRB to grant bargaining rights to faculties at just three private institutions between 1980 and 1999—American University's English Language Institute, Bradford College, and St. Thomas University (Leatherman, 1998a; Bronfenbrenner and Juravich, 2001). Indeed, in some cases, university faculty members have themselves made the argument that unionization and shared governance might not fit very well together. For instance, when Illinois State University's board of trustees stripped the academic senate of its power to make decisions concerning curricular issues in January 1998, many faculty members contemplated unionization. A group called Faculty Members for Shared Governance, however, countered that it would be more productive to work with the university administration and the board to alter its decision, as it did in 1999; a subsequent vote on a proposal to form a National Education Association–affiliated faculty union failed.

Yet the 1999 American Faculty Poll indicated that only 36.9 percent strongly agreed that faculty members were treated fairly, and only 45.4 percent strongly agreed that intrusions on academic freedom were rare (Sanderson, Phua, and Herda, 2000). At the same time, in the case of presidential evaluations, faculty representatives perceived a trend toward limiting faculty involvement and expanding the importance of patron-client politics in public university systems (Basinger, 1999a; Hamilton, 1999; AAHE, 2000). Extensive evidence suggests that the appropriate role of boards of trustees remains controversial. For instance, former Auburn University President William V. Muse told a faculty senate committee that despite his efforts to maintain authority over Auburn's athletics program, a committee of trustees had made all policy decisions directly for years (Suggs, 2001). Yet approximately a year later, a special Southern Association of Colleges and Schools–appointed investigator concluded that Auburn University's board of trustees was in compliance with accreditation standards related to governance, apart from a single case of "improper meddling" that resulted in the elimination of a doctoral program in economics (Pulley, 2002). Again, despite her continuing support by the faculty, the board of trustees forced Hollins University President Janet E. Rasmussen to step down as a result of her willingness to consider the admission of men, given declining enrollment. Remarkably, this incident occurred only a few months after she had been granted a five-year contract extension (Brownstein, 2001).

In yet another example, the faculty senate at George Mason University in May 2000 voted to censure the institution's governing board of visitors a day after the latter adopted a new set of general education requirements (Magner, 2000).

Facing the Fundamental Challenges

In sum, a number of fundamental challenges to effective governance occur within the prototypical university environment:

Too many constituencies take a seat at the academic table and claim a piece of the pie (Scott, 1997). Sometimes, agendas conflict. Who is the client? Who ultimately decides? Are the most important loyalties attached to the discipline or to the institution?

Philosophical views on the extent of inclusiveness and the optimal depth of consultation vary widely. Some consider inclusive consultation as necessary to advance discipline-based knowledge and student learning. Others see it as dangerous, because it leads to governance through multiple vetoes by campus groups with vested interests (de Russy, 1996).

The industry is rich with traditions and idiosyncrasies, as illustrated by the concept of tenure. In environments where tenured professors can exercise power but are not subject to any sanctions, there is often no sense of urgency to address pressing problems. Moreover, such freedom and autonomy without attendant costs, should errors of judgment occur, can serve to encourage academic leaders to execute top-down decisions (Sowell, 1994).

Multivariate differences in perspectives between faculty and administrators, faculty and trustees, and administrators and trustees can emerge, with levels of explicitness that might vary with time and the policy issue being addressed.

Governance from a Presidential Perspective

To be sure, effective university management is a straightforward process, in principle. What is required is an evaluation of external opportunities and competition, complemented by an assessment of internal resources, followed by the formulation of strategies derived from this analysis, and the implementation of a people-oriented plan of action. In practice, however, any given institutional structure frequently implies different layers of perspectives and expectations, which can greatly complicate each step. Presidential success in managing and leading institutions is often correlated with a combination of cognitive complexity and sensitivity, implying an ability to view an institution from a variety of perspectives, balancing structural, human relations, political, and symbolic concerns, to integrate and apply opposing ideas while responding to potential environmental threats in ways that also reflect values such as honesty, integrity, concern for academic principles, and interest in the role and progress of faculty members.

Birnbaum (1992) notes that each campus has its own unique governance system, which typically evolves idiosyncratically to fit individual leadership styles, personality mixtures, and organizational cultures. A new college president may be tempted to try to copy systems that appeared functional or particularly effective during his or her previous experience. But because nothing fails like success, this approach can have disastrous results.

In the case of such presidents, the tendency exists for the initial success and muted criticism of the honeymoon period to be followed by overestimated effectiveness, insensitivity to complaints, and diminished communication with the faculty. Because institutional problems are often related to resource acquisition or political support, presidents over time may communicate most with, and respond to, trustees and other administrators rather than faculty or students.

This trend may become self-reinforcing. Although trustees are most likely to assess presidents based on their perceived competence and commitment and administrators to focus on competence and involvement, faculty are often more concerned with the president's respect for their views and for institutional culture (Fujita, 1990). If total agreement between president and board is neither to be expected nor essential, the relationship is paradoxical, as presidents are hired to carry out trustees' policy directives, while at the same time, trustees look to the president for guidance and institutional leadership.

Conflicts between the board and the president or loss of confidence by the board has been cited as the prime reason for presidential resignations (Birnbaum, 1992). Substantial evidence suggests, however, that, especially for university presidents, successful tenures in office are most likely when they are seen to seek continuous input from the faculty and to support faculty participation in the governance process. For instance, a comparative case study of thirty-two institutions of higher education found that failed presidents were those who most frequently lost faculty support early in their tenures, while exemplary presidents tended to manage the retention of such support throughout their terms of service (Birnbaum 1990). Even given faculty support, however, there is no shortage of potential trip wires, as exemplified by presidents who attempt to resolve crises without an effective communications plan (Ross and Halstead, 2001; Schoenfeld, Weimer, and Lang, 1997; Larson, 1994).

Evolving Issues in the Twenty-First-Century University

Universities of the twenty-first century will face challenges not readily compared with any experienced in the history of the academy. The future of the professoriat, the composition of future faculties, and the impact of environmental demands on higher education remain unclear, although some may argue that they are not really new challenges. An aging faculty, the impact of technology and its associated costs, the increasing political pressure to measure outcomes, and the ubiquitous information explosion are all factors that will have significant effects on all educational levels, from pre-K through graduate and professional schools.

Perhaps one of the more complex evolving challenges to university governance arises from the aging of the faculty (Springer, 2001). Approximately one-third of all U.S. professors are fifty-five or older, up from about one-quarter just ten years ago. While less than 1 percent of university professors are older than seventy, only about one-third of all faculty members are younger than forty-five. In some fields, this phenomenon will have a tremendous effect, given an already tight job market, and will increasingly impact university campuses as the baby boomers age.

The greatest increase in faculty age groups has been in the fifty-five- to sixty-five-year-old cohort, while the largest decrease occurred in those thirty-five to forty-four years old. Faculty development and subsequent recruitment are not uniform across disciplines. Some departments in the humanities such as English and history find abundant applicants, while others such as computer science, accounting, engineering, and business find the applicant pool relative to demand very small. This competition results in higher salary disparities between professors of different disciplines, with obvious effects on faculty members' morale.

Another dramatic change that has occurred nationwide is the increasing dependence on part-time faculty and adjuncts. During 1970 to 1993, the number of full-time higher education faculty grew by 47 percent, to 546,000, but the number of adjunct professors increased 353 percent, to 370,000 (National Center for Education Statistics, 1997). Although generally deploring the use of so many adjuncts, full-time faculty members tend to exacerbate the problem by not wanting to teach entry-level courses. By teaching small, upper-level specialty courses and by engaging in what can be seen by the general public as superfluous research, faculty may fail to generate support among donors or legislatures. This situation in turn can lead to what faculty view as interference by governing board and political interests. At the same time, adjunct faculty members, who may hold several teaching positions at different institutions, are less likely to be involved in the campus governance process, which both increases the need for participation on the part of full-time faculty and potentially weakens the voice of the faculty in general.

A Port for Every Pillow

It has already been noted that the dramatic perceived increase in higher education costs has generated significant public interest. Perhaps no single source of skyrocketing expenses is more apparent than that seen in the technology area. What could be done thirty years ago with paper and pencil now requires a computer, complete with a laser printer, a scanner, and a dedicated Internet connection. And not just any computer: it must be new and fast with all the latest peripherals. The challenge of connecting the campus to the Internet is daunting and expensive, and the drive to be among the most wired led many colleges to spend millions of dollars on hard wiring their dorms and classrooms. "A port for every pillow" became the rallying cry across campuses. And immediately on the heels of this wiring came the demand for wireless connections, with increased mobility and at expanded cost.

Accordingly, many universities and colleges have begun to provide computers for all their students. Wake Forest University was among the first to do so. In an excellent example of shared governance, faculty and administrators collaborated in making this decision within a policy framework provided by trustees. Students bear the cost of laptops and related support services. Other universities have provided their students with the exact specifications for the computers they should bring to campus in an effort to avoid constant upgrades for their on-campus machines.

The evolving effects of educational technology on stakeholders' perceptions are just beginning to be seen, however. Who would have imagined in 1980, just before the introduction of the personal computer, that classroom presentations and discussions would be so influenced by bits and bytes? Technology will certainly continue to expand as an integral component of classroom instruction (Van Dusen, 1997). One can easily forget that the Internet did not really exist, for all practical purposes, as late as in 1990. Senior faculty often find it particularly challenging to use multimedia Internet resources, various software programs, and rapidly changing hardware to good effect (Webber, 1997). The proliferation of educational technology and its effective integration into the teaching and learning process naturally have even more impact on teaching and learning methodologies, and on students themselves, in institutions located outside North America and Europe.

Technology has more subtle influences on students' expectations. Marketing research indicates that the attention span of the typical adolescent is eleven minutes, which coincidentally is the typical time between commercials. Video games and active hands-on educational techniques have created their own set of problems for teachers. Today's faculty members often feel the need to keep up with, or be left behind by, the fast pace of change.

Clark Kerr, first chancellor of the University of California at Berkeley and later its president, once observed that of the approximately eighty-five institutions in the western world that had been established before 1520 and still existed with unbroken history and similar function, seventy were universities. With some ten centuries of tradition, is it any wonder that universities have been traditionally viewed as stable institutions? The fundamental elements of colleges and universities have long been seen as the collegiate faculty, the campus as a place for learning, the chosen student body, the library, and face-to-face instruction. Yet today, increasingly competitive higher education institutions exist without any of these characteristics (Newman, 2000).

The ability to recognize and respond to environmental change is essential for college and university stakeholders, especially faculty, administrators, and trustees. *Scholarship Assessed: Evaluation of the Professoriate* (Glassick, Huber, and Maeroff, 1997) contained only *one* reference to technology. The impact that communications technology would have on faculty roles and rewards was not anticipated. But this impact is here and now, and colleges and universities must face the question Can the necessary organizational learning occur?

Organizational Learning, Leadership, and Change

The concept of organizational learning is still relatively new. It is often indispensable for changing an institution and improving its performance. But not everyone in any given university is ready for change, and it is always the case that some do not perceive change as positive. Some learning is adaptive. College and university stakeholders react to the changing environment around them with differential levels of enthusiasm and engagement. For instance, some faculty members might adopt e-mail and online syllabi, but the fundamental way in which they teach and conduct themselves might remain rooted in their experience as students and young educators.

Others may be more willing to develop new techniques, explore new technologies such as Lotus Notes or WebCT, and experiment with methods of improving learning. This proactive learning can move well beyond simple reactions to incremental environmental change. The challenge to stable university cultures is to learn to adjust missions and goals, processes and procedures, in the light of change in the higher education environment. This change must be made relatively quickly, given the cumulative changes that have already occurred.

Leadership is key to managing change. It is often helpful to remind ourselves that change can occur at any level, formally or informally. Collective leadership may be just as important as executive leadership. A leader is truly only as good as the people attracted to work with him or her. As the learning curve progresses, several principles might be recalled when seeking to encourage organizational learning.

In any organization, workers naturally fear any change imposed on them. Change is most effective when each person makes his or her own decision about why, what, when, and how to change. Administrators sometimes forget to treat faculty as equal participants in the process. Faculty prefer to be regarded as significant stakeholders, not as subordinates who are expected to do what they are told. Given reliable and accurate information and the freedom to make their own choices, most faculty members will choose continuous improvement in their work as a matter of self-satisfaction. It continues to be insufficiently recognized that for many faculty members, the intrinsic rewards of doing a good job and securing recognition far outweigh the actual or potential material gains that accrue from work (Schick, Novak, Norton, and Elam, 1993).

A clearly defined vision of the desired end result helps identify the critical path to get there. Sometimes the path actually taken may be the most efficient; other times it may simply be the path of least resistance. But the more input faculty have in defining the changes and understanding how the changes will affect their work, the more likely they are to assume ownership, because with participation and involvement, trust is built. Building trust within the institution is critical to overall success. This trust can be earned only by a clear vision that is shared by the community, meaningful values that are plainly articulated and that authentically represent the community, and a credible link between words and actions on the part of academic leaders.

It is notoriously hard to hit a moving target. But as any marksman knows, one can learn from one's mistakes. Organizational learning in today's rapidly evolving dot.com world occurs when we scan the environment, make decisions, evaluate the results, adjust practices as necessary, and again evaluate observed outcomes, including the effectiveness of new methodologies in contributing to institutional mission. Each organization needs to decide collectively where it is going and what it is going to do when it gets there. In the case of universities, we contend that organizational learning facilitates common perspectives and shared expectations, thus creating the conditions for a mutually supportive approach to governance.

The George Mason Case

In 1999, the Association of Governing Boards of Universities and Colleges reiterated its view that the ultimate responsibility for an institution rested with its governing board, adding that commonly accepted business standards should inform academic management (Association of Governing Boards, 1999). At the same time, in forty-eight states, higher education governing or coordinating boards assumed at least some superordinate legal management and control responsibilities (Richardson, Bracco, Callan, and Finney, 1998). Tensions between governing boards and faculty have evinced themselves even in curricular matters, with George Mason University as a repeated case in point (Magner, 1999).

George Mason University, a relatively young institution by academic standards, was established in 1957 as a branch of the University of Virginia. It became an independent school in 1972. By the late 1990s, the faculty was accusing the board of visitors of micromanaging the university, especially on academic issues. The faculty felt that the president did not represent their interests to the board. The board moved in spring 1999 to reorganize the university, but with very little faculty input. Tension developed because the board of visitors perceived that George Mason's faculty senate was creating a nightmare of bureaucratic obstacles to reorganization. Applying a typical corporate model, the board wanted to reorganize and move on. The faculty senate wanted to make sure the board heard the views of the faculty, while the board wanted to make sure the faculty understood that the trustees would not rubber-stamp the faculty senate's views.

Several separate issues drove the controversy at George Mason. One was who controls academic credit, a second was the fate of the university's experimental New Century College. New Century College was a nontraditional, interdisciplinary program, independent of the more traditional College of Arts and Sciences. In the first case, the faculty senate had voted to award ten credits for eight military science courses, only to be overruled by the board, which voted to award twelve to eighteen credits. The board also voted to ask the university administration to eliminate the New Century College program and combine it with the College of Arts and Sciences. A faculty committee had recommended continuation of the college for another five years, while the faculty senate itself, the official faculty governing body, had not been asked for its opinion.

The George Mason case is a classic illustration of how and why governance often remains contested between faculty, administrators, and board members. Perceptions of shared governance vary. Expectations of involvement have yet to be standardized (Twale and Shannon, 1996). Inevitably, therefore, the structure and process of university governance continue to be controversial at many higher education institutions across the world.

The Case of the Institutes of Business at the University of the West Indies

In higher education institutions across the world, attempts have been made to create hybrid centers, institutes, and programs designed to escape the traditional governance systems of universities and to facilitate greater autonomy in decision making, financial independence, and more effective responses to the market.

These attempts can be most clearly seen in business schools in most countries. Such schools often operate as autonomous or semiautonomous institutions within university communities. Business schools themselves contain quite diffuse arrangements to ensure the effective management and delivery of specific programs such as full-time, part-time, and modular MBAs. Moreover, the same business school may contain a range of executive programs or shorter, intensive courses of modular design, which might be separately or differently managed. In some institutions, the business school is hardly linked to the rest of the university by more than name and institutional affiliation, as with the Stern School of Business at New York University or the Warwick Business School at Warwick University.

An issue of some contention stemming out of this situation is that significant salary differentials often favor business school academic staff or faculty.

In some institutions, especially in areas of high demand or significant need, other university units, for instance, schools of education, have adopted the model pioneered by business schools. Some even argue that the market-driven governance model of business schools has had some impact on the rethinking of approaches to university governance, tending to move universities in the direction of a more business-like approach to the delivery and management of education.

At each of the three main campuses of the University of the West Indies—Jamaica, Trinidad, and Barbados—executive education and custom-designed training programs as well as business consultancy services were separated entirely from the traditional departments of management studies, which became focused mainly, but not exclusively, on undergraduate business education. New institutions called Institutes of Business (in the case of the campus in Barbados, the Center for Management Studies) were created in 1989 to deliver innovative education, training, and consultancy programs and services. It was an entrepreneurial initiative by the University of the West Indies in partnership with the local private sector, which provided the seed money to get the new units off the ground. Private sector representatives hold the majority of the places on the boards of directors and, as stakeholders, constitute their principal client bases. Although the university is responsible for ensuring quality control, the institutes of business have autonomous control of their finances, are required to ensure a surplus of income over expenditure, and pay for services provided by the university. Since the early 1990s, the institute of business at the university campus in Trinidad has seen particularly significant growth in number of students and services offered in the marketplace and is on its way to sustainable profitability while fulfilling its articulated mission of generating intellectual capital by delivering quality educational services to stakeholders and by undertaking studies and research in areas of strategic importance for the sustainable economic growth and development of the Caribbean region.

The University of the West Indies created the institutes of business to provide more responsive and relevant business education programs during the economic liberalization period of the 1980s as a result of unfulfilled private sector demand. The institutes provided a valuable and significant solution to the structural, political, and symbolic dilemma confronted by the university. But even today, influential voices at the university contend that the institutes of business should never have been created, given the prior existence of at least emergent graduate business schools within the traditional governance structure. This case underscores the fact that tensions between concepts of governance persist and are not readily resolved, abroad as well as within the United States. As many opinions about ideal governance structures and processes remain as individuals willing to articulate their views.

Governance: State and Campus Surveys

The results of two surveys completed in 1998 and 1999 further demonstrate that such divergences cannot be simply wished or waved away.

A survey by Richardson, Bracco, Callan, and Finney (1998) explored state-level governance. The authors reviewed seven state systems of higher education and found that tensions emerged among various players as the states, regardless of their governing styles and objectives, sought to balance market demands and institutional or professional values. They found that a system was most effective in achieving its state-identified goals when its policy-making environment, its system design (structure, mission, capacity), and its work processes (information management, budget advice, planning, and collaboration) functioned in tandem. Clearly, therefore, the challenges of alignment and synergy are not to be underestimated.

In 1999, Immerwahr examined governance from within the campus. In a survey of 601 professors, higher education deans and administrators, government officers, and business leaders across the country, he determined that major disputes persisted regarding how well colleges and universities were administered, the content of the curriculum, and the cost of higher education. The majority of all respondents agreed that political infighting between and among faculty and administrators represented a serious problem and that, too often, colleges were run by highly bureaucratic administrations that resist change and progress. The survey also documented significant agreement regarding the value of higher education, both to society and to individuals. Thus, even when a community can agree on the value and significance of what it does, some minimum shared understanding as to how it should be done must still be present to facilitate excellence.

In 2001 and 2002, the National Center for Postsecondary Improvement (NCPI) published a three-part report that focused on the various stakeholder groups: recent college graduates, the public, and employers (National Center for Postsecondary Improvement, 2001a, 2001b, 2002), each reflecting the results of a survey done by NCPI. The survey was an attempt to find out how well the U.S. higher education system is working.

The first report, on recent college graduates, concerned responses obtained from students who received baccalaureate degrees from accredited institutions between 1991 and 1994 (National Center for Postsecondary Improvement, 2001a). The answer to a basic question—What do you know?—was somewhat encouraging: approximately two-thirds (63 percent) felt confident they could organize and communicate information to others, and almost as many (61 percent) were comfortable with their quantitative skills. Only 48 percent of the graduates in the sample, however, felt they had the ability to do research on a given topic.

The message from the public, the subject of the second report, gave colleges and universities a solid B. Those surveyed rated higher education better than high school, but only by a slim margin. These perspectives of stakeholders raised questions about the tensions between equal opportunity and self-reliance and about cost and efficiency in colleges today. And although the overall message is one of general satisfaction, the public believes that higher education should be held accountable for student learning.

The third part of the report drew its conclusions from employers of college graduates, the majority of whom believed that colleges and universities were doing their jobs. Employers were satisfied that graduates met the skill requirements necessary to do their jobs. The summary of the report series recommends that colleges and universities begin to plan for change. Although it is satisfying that the general perception of higher education is positive, academic leaders remain responsible for anticipating change as an inevitable element of the future.

One problem with any survey of U.S. higher education is the major variations found across state systems, which has led to interest in evaluating the performance of each state's colleges and universities. The National Center for Public Policy and Higher Education in 2001 issued what amounted to a report card for each state (see Callan, Doyle, and Finney, 2001). This report card examined individual states in relation to preparation, participation, affordability, completion, and benefits. Although certain gaps exist in the available data and discussion, the report constitutes a highly informative study of higher education in the United States.

Toward a More Effective System

Reference was repeatedly made during the 1990s in the popular literature to the emergence of a "new university," one that was shaped by market forces, administrative entrepreneurship, faculty creativity, and new approaches to governance (*Business Week,* June 25, 1997). This new university would be highly dependent on information technology, which was expected to increasingly promote decentralized responsibility, accountability, authority, and inclusiveness in universities. Such ideal governance systems would set priorities, focus missions, and implement choices, not merely create winners and losers (Benjamin and Carroll, 1998), and would establish environments where the sharing of authority would not necessarily diminish authority (Edelstein, 1997). How is such a model to be designed, developed, and executed? Perhaps a first step might be to understand the perceptions and attitudes of those entrusted to implement this process in particular institutions and to identify areas of intersection and divergence.

Governance: Attitudes and Perceptions

In an effort to expand understanding of the perceptions shared by faculty, administrators, and trustees, a group of American Council on Education fellows surveyed three cohorts of institutions during spring 1998: research and doctoral universities, comprehensive universities, and baccalaureate colleges. Provosts, vice presidents for academic affairs or chief academic officers, and faculty senate or council presidents at all universities in each category were invited to respond to the survey. The investigators mailed out five hundred sets of survey questionnaires to faculty leaders and senior administrators across these institutional categories.

The excellent response rate pointed to the high level of importance respondents assign to issues of governance. The group secured forty-five responses from administrators and thirty from faculty from research and doctoral institutions, with thirty from the same university; 155 responses from administrators and eighty-one from faculty from comprehensive institutions, with forty-two from the same university; and 166 responses from administrators and 100 from faculty from baccalaureate institutions, including sixty pairs.

The survey questionnaire contained twelve statements, formulated following an extensive literature survey (see Appendix B). The intent was to identify the characteristics of an ideal governance system based on the elements upon which administrators and faculty members could agree. The questions addressed the scope of decentralization, the match between authority and accountability, the effects of governance structure upon teaching and learning, the flexibility of the structure, and the effects of organizational culture and technology at each college or university. For each statement, respondents used a scale of 0–5 to submit two rankings, respectively indicating *perceived intrinsic importance* and *level of agreement*. The analysts computed averages and standard deviations for each statement within the three categories of institutions and the two types of respondents on both rankings. This process allowed for the measurement of the relative uniformity and value of each reaction as well as the effects of outliers. It was then possible to further segment the scale into three groupings—positive, neutral, and negative. They again computed averages and standard deviations, and evaluated response percentages within each group.

Faculty leaders and vice presidents for academic affairs reacted to these assertions by ranking the importance of these issues as factors that affect governance from insignificant to very significant, and rendering their opinions as to how well these affirmations described the state of governance at their institutions, from strong disagreement to strong agreement. Taken as a group, the responses offered four principal conclusions:

There seemed to be uniformity between and among faculty leaders and vice presidents for academic affairs regarding the important elements of university governance, such as collaboration between faculty and administrators and the enhancement of teaching and learning.

Faculty leaders and vice presidents for academic affairs recognized that the existing governance models at their colleges and universities fell short of their expectations. In fact, their collective responses indicated that the current system was much less functional than desired, but there was little uniformity as to the exact nature of the problem or the remedy required.

Perspectives across institutions, but especially at doctoral and research universities, clearly diverged regarding the value of decentralization and effects of hierarchy in governance.

At baccalaureate and comprehensive institutions, the perspectives of administrators were better aligned with those of faculty than they were at doctoral and research institutions.

The research reached the following conclusions:

Perceptions About Governance. Agreement was general across all institutions about the role of faculty in the governance process. Survey respondents listed areas where faculty members rather than administrators should have primary roles. The top four areas offered by most participants, without prompting from the survey, included curriculum, academic policies, tenure/promotion, and other personnel issues such as faculty recruitment and conditions of employment. Other items included by respondents covered the gamut from articulation agreements to scheduling and from student life to diversity.

Enhancing Learning and Teaching. The data showed that a relatively high percentage of faculty leaders at baccalaureate (77 percent) and comprehensive (80 percent) institutions assigned high rankings to the significance of teaching and learning as a focus for governance. In contrast, only about 65 percent of faculty leaders at doctoral and research universities considered learning and teaching "important" to "very important." Among vice presidents for academic affairs, a majority of those at comprehensive (80 percent) and baccalaureate (83 percent) institutions and half (50 percent) the total number at doctoral and research institutions shared the same view. In all cases, a clear majority expressed the belief that governance should enhance teaching and learning.

Information Technology. Most faculty leaders agreed that management information systems should make information widely available to all those who need and want it but that the expectation surpassed the reality. A much smaller group stated that it was already happening. These observations can be interpreted in several ways. Perhaps the technology is in place but not accessible to all interested faculty members. Alternatively, the technology may be accessible to faculty, but they might not think the right information is being shared in a timely manner. Or the technology might yet be unavailable on campus. From one-third to approximately one-half the faculty, across all institutions, indicated that technology has helped with information sharing at their universities.

Decentralized Budgeting and Governance. Most respondents did not perceive a direct link between budgetary issues and the governance process. The potentials of responsibility-centered management systems (discussed more fully later) elicited limited enthusiasm. One of the characteristics of responsibility-centered management types of decentralized budgetary systems is that they make fiscal and strategic planning more open and accessible to the university community, compared with traditional incremental budgeting systems (Whalen, 1991). For example, cost centers such as libraries and revenue centers such as academic colleges and schools present their fiscal plans to each other as part of the annual campus budget submission and approval cycle. A majority of the faculty at all institutions agreed with the proposition that the principles associated with decentralized budgeting contributed to shared university governance. Respondents at doctoral and research institutions, however, held a positive view of this relationship more strongly than those at baccalaureate and comprehensive universities. Further, although approximately the same proportion of senior academic administrators and faculty leaders agreed with the principle that decentralized budgeting enhances shared governance, a larger and more uniform proportion of administrators indicated that responsibility-centered management and governance were insignificantly related.

Organizational Culture. An internal interaction between organizational culture and governance makes it difficult to disentangle these factors and leaves a great deal of room for individual interpretation. Nevertheless, a large majority of faculty leaders and vice presidents for academic affairs across all three categories of institutions indicated that the organizational culture was, in principle, a major catalyst for, or constraint on, shared governance (see Appendix C). But far fewer faculty leaders and senior administrators were prepared to say whether or not they perceived it as being the case on their campuses. It is noteworthy that administrators and faculty in the same institutional category agreed on this issue, more than any other. If academic leaders also agree that governance arrangements should enhance the process of teaching and learning, the most effective approaches and best practices remain to be addressed, the subject of the following chapter.

Emphases Emerging from the Literature

What additional evidence is available about the current perceptions concerning university governance held by higher education leaders? The bibliography of this volume reflects the concerns and issues identified in the literature as being the most common. Before beginning to write, we identified a number of significant issues, primarily by content analysis of the literature. The bibliography reflects research conducted at this stage. Further, survey research has shown that faculty, administrators, and trustees view these concerns and issues as significant.

To be sure, the underlying attitudes of individual faculty leaders, administrators, and trustees toward institutional governance are not as readily ascertained as might be imagined. Yet considerable literature is available on the topic. One reason is that although not all members of the attentive audience fully understand the issues and their implications, everyone evidently has an opinion.

The major concerns reflected in the bibliography include the legal issues that surround institutional governance. Although this aspect of college and university governance is not as extensively represented in the bibliography as in the case of faculty's, administrators', and trustees' attitudes toward governance, legal opinions relevant to higher education continue to accumulate. That this issue is of great concern to all sectors of higher education is unsurprising. American society has made the legal system the accepted and almost expected means of deciding a very wide range of problems and disagreements.

Perhaps the most reassuring finding to emerge from an examination of the literature is that most faculty, administrators, and boards of trustees are genuinely interested in enhancing teaching and learning (Chait, 2000). Boyer's *Scholarship Reconsidered* focused attention on this subject in 1990, and Glassick, Huber, and Maeroff's *Scholarship Assessed* attracted further attention in 1997. The very concept that a scholarship of teaching and learning exists continues to have a positive impact on higher education. The role of governance in that scholarship, however, is not as well articulated.

Meanwhile, the impact of educational technology and the subsequent emergence of distance education (e-learning) has continued to grow. But the concerns of the various sectors of higher education differ somewhat. Faculty members want the newest and fastest technology and the training to use it effectively. Administrators want a way to use technology efficiently, and to improve teaching and learning and faculty productivity. Boards of trustees want to know how to fund expanding technology applications.

Discussion of the finances and costs of higher education is also well represented in the literature. This subject has impelled serious discussions about accountability, which in turn have generated extensive conversations about governance, including budgetary issues such as responsibility-centered management. One additional subject remains to be addressed: organizational culture. Organizational culture is the cumulative result of multiple attitudes and values that accrete within an individual institution, and the size, academic nature, and function of any given college or university directly impact how governance evolves.

Universities are often viewed as institutions that are administered, managed, and led in a hierarchical fashion, with organizational structures akin to a pyramid. From the perspective of the delivery of education to students in a teaching and learning community by competent professionals, however, the structure of the prototypical university may be argued to be relatively flat, as all courses are delivered in academic units and a great deal of program management and even leadership takes place within these units. A distinction might be made between the infrastructures for systemic decision making and for educational program delivery. The decision-making style and culture of the university, the infrastructures that supports both processes, and the operationalization strategies implemented interact to determine the extent to which each institution is able to create value for its stakeholders.

Governance and Teaching and Learning

WE HAVE POSITED THAT GOVERNANCE is the structure and process of authoritative decision-making across issues that are significant for external and internal stakeholders. For colleges and universities, no issue is more central than the relationship between such structures and processes and the internal environment for teaching and learning.

The Environmental Context for Education

The extent to which campus stakeholders perceive institutional governance to be shared can enhance or constrain the role of a college or university as a vehicle for teaching and learning. A provocative Matt Hall cartoon in the *Chronicle of Higher Education* (November 24, 2000, p. B20) neatly encapsulates the potential clash of perceptions in teaching and learning: a classroom teacher sees a flock of sleeping or literally thoughtless sheep, who in turn see an owlish authority figure presenting meaningless gibberish. If it is widely accepted that institutional governance should enhance learning and teaching, how can it be that so many faculty and administrators question whether governance arrangements at their own universities actually contribute effectively to this end?

Faculty members and administrators often continue to work in individual silos, which is one of the key underlying issues. Richard Breslin tells the story of how, several decades ago, when he was assuming his first administrative appointment as the dean of a college of arts and sciences, the outgoing dean breakfasted with him. The former expressed pleasure at once again assuming the mantle of "we" and warned that the latter was about to become one of "them." In fact, both sides suffer from restricted fields of vision, as administrators are often removed from the day-to-day business of teaching and learning and faculty may fail to see beyond their classrooms or disciplines (Breslin, 2000).

Stuart Rojstaczer (1999) contends that the quality of teaching and learning has declined, especially in research-oriented universities, and that grade inflation has increased for a range of reasons, among them enrollment expansion incentives, tuition increases, the pressure for faculty to publish and pursue grants, the impact of institutional athletics programs, and students' reduced expectations. This chapter defines effective teaching and learning, then demonstrates how some of the main environmental components at a prototypical university—mission and goals, size, constituents served, visibility, culture, climate, and programmatic range—impact the potential for such teaching and learning, both directly and indirectly.

Teaching can be enhanced by internally aligning objectives, teaching methods, and assessment tasks (Biggs, 1996). In any given class, each student's academic orientation and level of engagement interact with the kind of learning activity that a particular teaching method stimulates. Student engagement can range from simply memorizing facts and taking notes through relating and applying material to independent reflection and theorizing (Biggs, 1999).

Larry Spence argues that it is impractical to expect significantly improved university teaching until professors become designers of "learning experiences" rather than teachers in the traditional sense. Teaching is an instinctive and unconscious human activity, which becomes evident when we observe adults, regardless of culture, engaging babies in communication. Such communication, however, is implicitly premised on one-on-one relationships. Every step up in scale decreases effectiveness (Tuckman, 1994). Further, because the human brain represents rather than records reality and curiosity catalyzes learning, individuals infrequently link large-scale classroom teaching to the experienced world (Heywood, 2000). Indeed, knowledge transfer between disciplines, from one classroom to the next, is a continual challenge. One result is that many university graduates cannot formulate and solve work-relevant problems, cooperate effectively with other team members in high-stress situations, or write and speak forcefully and persuasively. By contrast, curious students constantly log on to the Internet to learn, in an active and adaptive manner (Spence, 2001).

Indeed, learning is not an issue of imposed or transmitted meaning. Learning occurs best when specific learning activities are designed, implying a "deep" rather than "surface" approach. To take advantage of this approach, students need the relevant background knowledge and intrinsic curiosity or a desire to do well, as well as the ability to grasp and manipulate concepts (Argyris, 1991; Biggs, 1996).

At the same time, teaching is most effective when impelled by reflective efforts to communicate the intrinsic structure of a topic or subject in depth while encouraging high expectations of success, providing sufficient time for each task, and rewarding "relational learning" in the process of assessment (Gray, 1991). Real understanding is performance based in that learning changes not only students' perspectives but also their ability to put this new understanding into practice, in a specific and pragmatic way (Brown and Knight, 1994). This situation is analogous to the conceptual leap from a grasp of theoretical principles to their successful application. From an educator's perspective, the encouragement of effective or active learning is a low-risk strategy with high returns. Active inquiry should pervade the curriculum of any institution that is committed to provide an excellent education (Blimling and Whitt, 1999).

Organizational Culture and Learning

In 1999, the American Association for Higher Education used the theme Organizing for Learning: Constant Values, Competitive Contexts to examine the future of higher education. What questions will shape the scholarship of higher education in the early twenty-first century? One of the questions asked on campuses around the world is whether most, if not all, students can achieve intense educational engagement and relational learning. Can such learning occur within established university cultures? In the name of enhanced learning, trustees, senior administrators, and even peers impel faculty to reach out continually to their students by applying new pedagogies and by using the most innovative teaching techniques effectively.

Faculty members have often felt that a focus on the core values of academic freedom and shared governance would facilitate greater access to education for all students while encouraging effective teaching. But how are values such as quality, liberal learning, diversity, and a sense of community actually embodied in alternative pedagogies and structures? For example, does the use of service-learning actually increase a student's engagement in his or her own education? What about concepts such as learning communities or problem-based learning? In many ways, the organizational culture and the governance of the university determine just how much these approaches can engage their students in a way that will better equip them to function in a complex, interdependent world.

Organizational cultures and climates have continued to engage academic interest and debate (Cooper, Cartwright, and Early, 2001). The curriculum, teaching methods and assessment procedures used, classroom climate created, and broader institutional environment are all critical components of teaching, which cumulatively affect the potential for students' learning and real understanding. In turn, the effectiveness of all strategies for improving teaching can be enhanced or adversely affected by the nature of the organizational culture in which these strategies are implemented.

Organizational cultures that are conducive to teaching and learning include several characteristics:

- The commitment of senior administrators and department chairs to reward good teaching as well as research;
- Faculty who value teaching and are collaboratively engaged in planning as well as implementing programs to improve teaching, thereby creating ownership of these activities;
- Tenure and promotion processes that are directly connected to rigorous evaluations of teaching (Massy, Wilger, and Colbeck, 1994; Rice and Austin, 1988).

The Carnegie Foundation for the Advancement of Teaching now includes ten categories of colleges and universities, ranging from doctoral/research universities—extensive or intensive—to master's colleges and universities to baccalaureate colleges (liberal arts or general or associate) to specialized institutions and tribal colleges and universities. These institutions vary in size and governance mechanisms, student profiles, historical development, types and levels of degrees offered, range of programs, instructional delivery systems, and administrative processes. These factors naturally affect institutional culture, climate, and visibility. The key issue here is one of implicit as well as explicit incentives: How do such factors interact to affect faculty and student motivation, respectively, to teach and to learn, applying best practices?

The relationship between effective teaching and learning and these elements of the institutional environment can be readily outlined. Culture and climate are particularly important, while good teaching might be viewed simply as the possession of appropriate competencies such as curriculum development, classroom management, the integration of instructional technologies, and equitable student evaluation, translating into positive student feedback. The remainder of this chapter discusses the impact of institutional size, student profiles, and program range as well as institutional history of educational engagement.

Institutional Size

Although baccalaureate universities and liberal arts colleges may be able to offer small classes and an attractive faculty-student ratio to all their students, classes in large universities are often relatively large, apart from honors and other special academic enrichment programs. Such classes are typically taught by lectures, which can communicate information and interpretations rather readily but tend to limit faculty-student interaction in class and to demand a great deal of concentration from students.

Further, large lecture classes do not readily stimulate a deep approach or relational learning and are unlikely to inspire students or to change their attitudes toward any particularly challenging subject matter in a positive manner. Periodic pauses, changes in the pace and nature of classroom activity to clarify and elaborate lecture content, and active review by students accompanied by group projects, peer teaching, and the use of learning materials outside the classroom, however, can all enhance learning, even in large lectures (Biggs, 1999).

Many large institutions have adopted innovative practices in response to this challenge. For instance, Carnegie Mellon University has been implementing a recommendation made by two 1998 university task forces, one on broadening education and the other on creating extraordinary value for students. An "hourglass model" encapsulates these recommendations. Undergraduates broaden the range of their courses at the beginning and end of their four years while focusing on their core discipline in their middle years. In a somewhat similar spirit, Johns Hopkins encourages first-semester freshmen to explore their interests without the assignment of course letter grades. Until the second semester, students' performance is simply evaluated as "satisfactory" or "unsatisfactory."

At the University of California at Los Angeles, a 1994 faculty-student study group called for far-reaching reform of the general education curriculum, which led to the establishment of a general education cluster. Incoming freshmen were offered the option of enrolling in a one-year, team-taught, interdisciplinary course. Students attend lecture courses and small discussion sections or labs taught by senior faculty and graduate student teaching fellows from a number of different disciplines. In the third quarter, the same students enroll in one of several satellite seminars, dealing with topics related to the overall cluster theme. Each such theme is designed to strengthen the writing and critical-thinking skills of first-year students while introducing them to the research and ideas of "ladder faculty" and exposing them to inquiry-based learning and interdisciplinary study.

The Faculty Center for Teaching and Learning at North Carolina State University has defined inquiry-based learning as an array of classroom practices that promote student learning through guided, and increasingly independent, investigation of questions and problems for which there is no single answer. This investigation requires the ability to formulate good questions, identify and collect appropriate evidence, present and interpret results systematically, and formulate worthwhile conclusions. A variety of teaching strategies can encourage inquiry-based learning, including interactive lectures, discussion, teamwork, case studies, service-learning, simulation, fieldwork, and laboratories ("Building and Leading Successful Learning Communities," 2000). This method of teaching and learning is reminiscent of the saying that one can tell whether an individual is clever by his answers and whether he is wise by his questions.

Student Profiles

A student may be defined as anyone whom a teacher is trying to influence through the process of teaching. Students vary by age, gender, ethnic background, home country, or region of origin in the United States. "Traditional" students, eighteen to twenty-three years of age, are increasingly a minority of total student population. In 1989, this category already included only about one-sixth of the then 12.7 million college and university students (Davis, 1993).

One Stanford University study identified five different categories of students: careerists, intellectuals, strivers, unconnected, and other (Katchadourian and Boli, 1985). These students all attended the same institution but had quite different goals and orientations. More generally, where traditional students might be at the conformist, self-aware, or conscientious stages (Loevinger, 1976), older students typically move through sequences of provisional adulthood, settling down, midlife transition, and restabilization (Chickering and Havinghurst, 1981).

Student goals and orientations continue to vary significantly. For example, an August 1999 American Council on Education and UCLA Higher Education Research Institute survey indicated that in political orientation, 56.5 percent of freshmen were middle of the road, 20.8 percent liberal, and 18.6 percent conservative; 28 percent planned to end their studies with a bachelor's degree and 38.7 percent with a master's; 48 percent chose the college attended because of its academic reputation, 32.3 percent on the basis of available financial assistance, and 28.9 percent because of low tuition. The prior decision to go to college, however, was driven by the desire to get a better job (76.9 percent), make more money (74.6 percent), and gain a general education and appreciation of ideas (62 percent). At the same time, corporate employers seek conformist university graduates who display the executive virtues of imagination, historical perspective, initiative, independence, resolve, perseverance, diligence, and patience (Macedo, 1990).

Institutional governance arrangements and incentives matter here as well. For example, the effective engagement of conformists, still focused on external values and stereotypes, and conscientious students, more focused on self-respect and long-term goals, demands different teaching orientations from those for adults who are settling down or involved in midlife transition.

Responsive teaching may be further complicated by cross-cutting differences of gender, ethnicity, and socioeconomic status in the same classroom.

As higher education becomes more focused on learning outcomes rather than seat time, where students earn a degree upon completion of the requisite number of credit hours and the number of nontraditional providers multiplies, the value added by any given institution to each student's learning experience will become the critical independent variable. Students will then set the institutional agenda for teaching and learning and evaluate the extent to which they are systematically engaged in such higher-order thinking tasks as analysis and synthesis.

Range of Programs and Institutional History

The link between program range, institutional history, and teaching orientations is illustrated by a national award given annually to college and university professors in recognition of their teaching. The Council for Advancement and Support of Education and the Carnegie Foundation for the Advancement of Teaching provide the only such award. Each year, faculty members from four types of institutions—baccalaureate colleges, community colleges, master's universities, and doctoral institutions—are nominated for the honors. The number of nominees continues to grow. In 1999, the four professors who made the cut were selected from more than 400 nominees; in 2000, more than 500 faculty members were nominated.

When Professor Marilyn Repsher from Jacksonville University, a master's-level institution, was named Professor of the Year in 1999, she explained that her goal as a professor was to help undergraduates understand "the excitement, the beauty, the glorious ride that is mathematics." She was recognized because, as she commented, she had led an effort to alter the curriculum by "stopping the premature rush to abstraction" and "focusing on real-world applications of mathematical principles directly related to articulated student interests" (Schneider, 2000).

A similar situation occurred in November 2000, when College of Holy Cross Associate Professor of Physics Robert Garvey won the top prize for baccalaureate teaching. The prize was mainly the result of a first-year residential two-seminar learning community that Professor Garvey initiated, centering on the question, "How, then, shall we live?" approached from interdisciplinary perspectives. Similarly, another final award winner, Theater Professor Brad Baker of the Collin County Community College District in Plano, Texas, encouraged his students to realize that they have to keep asking a related question, "how best to live?" (Schneider, 2000).

Professors from much larger, doctoral-extensive or -intensive institutions also regularly earn these teaching awards. The common denominators consist of the innovative efforts of individual faculty to encourage deep and relational learning and the institutional support to do so. Such support has been driven by mission and institutional history and by the realization, among senior administrators, that the evolving educational environment required much more attention to teaching and learning.

In enhancing learning and individual student development, the key is not simply for faculty to teach more and better, as some legislators and academic administrators might have it, but to create conditions that motivate and inspire students to educationally purposive activities, both inside and outside the classroom. Such activities may be most successful when they instill an understanding that to be absolutely certain about anything, one must know everything or nothing about it. Meanwhile, governance mechanisms vary on several dimensions: the essential variable, for the present purpose, may be whether universities and colleges are viewed from the top as academic corporations or as institutions intended to foster innovative teaching and learning. We therefore hold, partly for this reason, that the nature of governance has a direct and very significant impact on the effectiveness of teaching and learning.

Governance, Information Technology, and Distance Education

E VERY UNIVERSITY AND COLLEGE that aspires to be competitive in the twenty-first century higher education environment is attempting to make the most effective use of information technology and distance education systems. This is yet another arena in which governance arrangements matter.

The Impact of Information Technologies

Robert Burnside reports that once, while participating on a panel discussing how MBA programs might better serve working adult students by moving online, he witnessed the following exchange. One of the panelists, the president of a for-profit online university, referred to faculty members as "content providers." A professor on the panel angrily responded, "I am *not* a content provider! I am an educator! I have been in education for twenty years. Proprietary, for-profit online institutions pretend to be educational institutions, but whether you actually provide real learning is very much in question."

The first speaker answered, "You are defining 'real learning' as something that can only happen in a traditional classroom. However, employees now demand just-in-time learning that speaks to their context on the job. This is a service that traditional universities are simply not providing" (Burnside, 2001, pp. 21–22). To be sure, traditional academic education focuses on the mastery of a body of knowledge, socialization, and learning how to learn, while training, often conducted in the workplace, emphasizes applied skills. Yet today's students and tomorrow's employees need both education and training.

Consider for a few moments the traditional characteristics of a college or university. It has a residential student body and offers a combination of graduate and undergraduate programs, along with various professional schools for medicine and law, for example. Although we can categorize some schools as national, most are regional or local in scope. They have a recognizable geographic service area within which they are known and from which they draw their students. These institutions have full-time faculty who exercise control over such issues as curricular design and degree requirements. Classes are conceived in terms of seat-time, with face-to-face instruction. Faculty can earn tenure through a well-defined process, requiring excellence in teaching, demonstrated development of a professional research program, and published scholarship. In the interests of support from institutional stakeholders, community and university service is part of the role of any university professor.

In addition to the human side of education are the physical and economic dimensions of college or university existence. A central library with extensive holdings of books and periodicals and a carefully landscaped campus have been standard components of the traditional university. Given the nonprofit status of such institutions the need for fundraising is incessant.

Most institutions of higher learning accept the need to participate in a recurring evaluation process led by regional accrediting bodies to assess organizational effectiveness and to remain recognized as a provider of high-quality education. We base accreditation mainly on input, process, and output measurements of such factors as expenditures per student, levels of library holdings, quality of physical facilities, faculty-student ratios, percentage of doctoral or terminally qualified faculty, number of student applications and subsequent acceptances, and budgetary stability. We look then to see whether students are retained and graduate, normally within four to six years, and attempt to determine whether they learned anything while in attendance.

New Models of Higher Education

Educational technology has become the driving force for several new models or concepts in higher education. A major new mission is the provision of educational and training opportunities for adult learners. Within this market, competitiveness clearly demands accessibility and convenience, reduced costs, and the application of course content to the workplace. Students are customers. Faculty members are facilitators. Institutions, often through continuing education schools, are providers. But it frequently remains unclear to traditional senior academic administrators how to link the missions of such schools or divisions most effectively to the mission of the university as a whole.

A more adult- and customer-oriented process has been emerging across the higher education landscape, most apparent in the for-profit sector. Whereas students come to campus at traditional universities, for-profit models go to the student. Although relatively stable and extensive curricula linking liberal arts with professional education are typical at traditional colleges and universities, the for-profit curriculum is market driven and adult oriented. But the most striking difference may be seen in the delivery methods. Traditional colleges and universities continue to use lecture-based instruction. Although professors may use multimedia and e-mail communication, individual professors control their classrooms and course content.

In for-profit institutions, individual faculty control gives way to typically standardized instruction at multiple locations, with greater focus on students' experiences. Such institutions replace full-time faculty with appropriate academic preparation and credentials by part-time faculty with professional experience. The University of Phoenix is the prime for-profit model. Jorge Klor de Alva, former president of the university, once described the education provided by his institution as a just-in-time experience. Students learn what they can apply immediately in a career. In contrast, traditional universities provide just-in-case education: most student learning is unrelated to immediate objectives or applications (Newton, 2000). Whereas faculty members are positioned as disciplinary experts, course designers, presenters, and student evaluators at a typical university, the Phoenix model identifies separate course design, delivery, and assessment experts and adopts a systems approach orchestrated to produce expected learning outcomes. The number of for-profit examples is expanding, such as Sylvan Learning Systems Incorporated, Strayer College, the DeVry Institute of Technology, and UNext.

In addition, an increasing number of universities and colleges have evolved from the correspondence school tradition to the systematic extension of their classrooms through the use of satellite, broadcast and cable television, compressed digital video, and compact disc technologies. These institutions include for-profit subsidiaries created by Duke, New York University, Babson College, UCLA, Columbia, and Cornell as well as Jones International University, which has applied for accreditation from the North Central Association; the American Open University, which focuses on Islamic Studies in association with Al-Azhar University in Egypt; and the Virtual University, where classes are taught by volunteer instructors and award credits for continuing education units. Yet other institutions have formed e-learning consortia, such as Universitas 21 and the Global Education Network. Some traditional universities such as Boston University, Dartmouth College, the Johns Hopkins University, and Washington University in St. Louis have become significant investors in private equity funds that are purchasing for-profit college companies. But the world of e-learning has also experienced dramatic failures. For instance, the University of Toronto decided to leave Universitas 21, finding that their missions were inconsistent. Virtual Temple University was closed in 2000, after operating for approximately one year. Nevertheless, estimates of the value of the online education market continue to expand, to $40 billion and beyond.

The number of Web sites and program offerings devoted to education and training are expanding almost exponentially. One Web site, About.com, offers a guide to 700 sites for distance learning. Meanwhile, the Web site eLearners.com announces on its home page, "Find over 24,000 online and distance learning courses, leading to 2,400 distance and e-learning degrees and certificate programs," and underscores that these opportunities are offered by 1,600 e-learning providers.

E-learning has the potential to create a phenomenon that goes far beyond anything experienced since the foundation of universities at Bologna, Oxford, and Prague in the eleventh century. Perhaps the printing press had a similar impact, but certainly not as rapidly or as broadly. And the attentive audience at least potentially interested in using this technology to acquire education is tremendous. Traditional colleges and universities see new sources of revenue in the evolving higher education market—money to pay for all the delayed maintenance, all the computers and connectivity, all the faculty development, and all the assorted wants and desires of demanding residential campuses.

By 2000, there were approximately 15.3 million traditional college-age students in the United States, a number that was expected to grow but not explode in the present decade. A spring 2001 Merrill Lynch report estimated that 2.2 million college students would be taking online courses by the following year, compared with 710,000 in 1998—a 210 percent increase—while choosing from more than 6,000 online courses delivered by 84 percent of all four-year colleges and universities (Konrad, 2001). And 40 percent of adults over 30 years of age study part-time, a number that may increase to 60 percent in the next ten years. Add to that number the 28 million adult learners who want to have some additional training or educational experience, and it is obvious that the potential market for e-learning is huge.

New educational technologies have generated their own terminology and literature. The *Journal of Asynchronous Learning Networks,* for example, began publication in the 1990s. The prototypical denotation of the term *distance education* has evolved from correspondence courses distributed and graded by mail into e-learning or Web-based learning, online coursework, and Internet-mediated distance learning. The evolution of educational technology continues to change the profile of higher education.

With the ease of use that such technologies offer, it was almost inevitable that competition would emerge from the corporate world to challenge established educational institutions. In this era of digital transfer, several new corporate-style institutions are emerging with what should be unsurprising speed. No longer are community colleges, residential colleges, comprehensive universities, and large research universities the only players. By 2000, for instance, $2.5 billion in private investment was directed to companies focused on e-learning, a 155 percent increase over 1999 levels (Bransten, 2001).

Further competition for the adult learner comes directly from large multinational companies such as Motorola, American Express, Xerox, McDonald's, and Disney, which have developed academic programs that have sought and achieved accreditation. Although most of these programs do not grant degrees, it is apparent from the level of corporate support provided that industry increasingly views the in-house training of employees as essential to future competitiveness.

Something of a hybrid model is also emerging through the partnership of industry with universities. This model allows each partner to leverage its respective strengths while avoiding the costly pitfalls of having to acquire the expertise available from its partners. For instance, a number of institutions, including George Washington University, Penn State, and Columbia University, joined with AT&T to provide new educational opportunities (Hanna, 1998).

Some organizations are taking advantage of recent changes in the labor market that demand competency certification. Software companies, with Microsoft the most successful example, offer certification programs in the use of their products. Other institutions such as New York's Regents College and Western Governors University are attempting to offer competency-based certifications. Whereas Regents College offers a complete baccalaureate degree program through examination, Western Governors University, which was formed in 1996 by the governors of thirteen western states, attempts to use faculty specialists to develop curricula and individual course assessment processes. The drive toward more effective student outcomes assessment is a common denominator.

Traditional colleges and universities have developed their own adult degree programs. Using e-learning support tools such as Blackboard and WebCT, universities are taking techniques from the on-campus classroom and applying them to adult learners. Accelerated classes condense the typical fifteen- to sixteen-week semester to five, seven, or ten weeks in the interests of increased convenience and access for adult students. Many colleges and universities now give credit for life experience, attempting to recognize work experiences students bring to the classroom, virtual or otherwise. Such credit is awarded for experiences and knowledge gained on the job through portfolio evaluation, testing, and one-on-one interviews.

The American Council on Education has developed the smart transcript, which awards academic credit for skills gained by military personnel while on active duty. Some experience and schooling can have direct application for math, engineering, and science credit. Other training, for example, in keyboarding and clerical work, is not generally recognized by transcript evaluators at colleges and universities. These changes have stimulated many debates on campus regarding the distinction between education and training. For example, can an adult really learn in five weeks what has traditionally taken an eighteen- to twenty-one-year-old fifteen weeks to master? An outcomes-based rather than input-, process-, or output-based approach to learning can help to clarify matters while facilitating the development and application of truly useful distinctions between individual competencies.

Governance Structures and Educational Technologies

To what extent, and how, can governance structures facilitate the effective incorporation of educational technology into institutional programs and their delivery systems and processes while ensuring that student, financial aid, human resources, and business databases communicate smoothly, linking structural and conversational data? In fall 2002, approximately one-tenth of all universities and colleges with annual operating budgets in excess of $100 million had implemented or were seeking to implement comprehensive and relatively expensive interactive software systems, such as PeopleSoft, SAP, or Banner. The goal was to achieve significant economies of scale and scope as well as real-time responses to what-if budgetary questions, whether at the academic unit, division, or institutional level. In many cases, installation required a complete redesign of budgetary systems, from payroll and financial aid to maintenance, accompanied by extensive staff training programs. In a number of cases, glitches had to be addressed repeatedly, even after extended installation periods. But the potential for enhanced management and governance continued to attract the attention of senior executives at institutions ranging from the University of Michigan, Case Western Reserve University, the University of Massachusetts, and Princeton University (PeopleSoft) to the University of South Dakota, Central Michigan University, California State University at Chico, and the University of Mississippi (SAP).

How have such technologies impacted curriculum delivery? In 1997, a formal plan for incorporating technology into the curriculum existed at only 25 percent of higher education institutions, and only 10 percent of classes used the World Wide Web (Oblinger and Rush, 2000). An emerging rule of thumb is that an institution should allocate up to 10 percent of its budget to information technology to stay current, but few universities can support such expenditures.

New production, delivery, and certification organizations have invaded the distribution of higher education courses. Given this competitive environment, a key challenge of "sited" education is to make the case for the value of in-person interaction with peers and faculty and for the benefits to be gained from having students present themselves at the same time and place repeatedly for such purposes. It also needs to be explained clearly and repeatedly why liberal education provides the core of what it means to be an educated person. Yet the traditional concept of shared governance often suggests the need for consensus, which in turn implies resistance to change.

Shared governance, however, is not necessarily an impediment to technological change, especially when institutional governance encourages information empowerment with a significant degree of decentralized but coordinated decision making. The distributed client–server model of computing characterized by individual client units, purchased applications, windowing, and the use of private local area networks or mixed private-public switched networks is giving way to network-centric computing. This style requires multisource hardware platforms, software subscriptions rather than purchase, and public switched infrastructure, wired as well as wireless. As generations of computer technology succeed each other with increasing rapidity, the inadequacy of the prototypical twentieth-century structure and process of authoritative university decision making comes into sharper relief.

The implementation of an effective information technology strategy actually implies new models of governance, administration, and management. In terms of governance, authoritative decision making needs to be delegated downward to the lowest competent level, normally the department or program, with clearly specified rewards for teams that achieve defined objectives. Such a strategy requires a relatively flat hierarchy, operational integration, and the celebration of a culture of achievement and service. Distributed online processing with common high-speed networking interfaces across college and university campuses can facilitate this approach (Katz and West, 1992). A single-system image, or natural extension of a given user's native computing environment free from specific computing and communications protocols, can create the kind of integrated systems architecture that can transform university administration (Gleason, 1991). Such changes, however, require the vision and commitment of trustees, presidents, and other senior university leaders, leading us back to the challenges to governance posed by e-learning.

From the perspective of university governance, the impact of technology has brought with it a new set of significant challenges. Who controls course content? Who sets the standards for faculty qualifications? How do we accredit these programs? The Council of Regional Accrediting Commissions, comprising the six regional accreditation bodies, hired the Western Cooperative for Educational Telecommunication to develop new standards for distance education programs (Carnevale, 2000). The council rather than each regional accrediting commission was charged with this task, because distance education programs have potentially unlimited geographical reach. The basic premise of the guidelines is to use technology to better understand the strengths and weaknesses of individual students and to focus on student learning. More and more institutions are joining with for-profit companies to offer online distance education courses, which can generate conflicts within governance structures on campus.

The for-profit model has been promoted as appropriate for colleges and universities in general. Many board members who come from a corporate background view education as a product and want to govern its "production." From this perspective, it is inefficient and cumbersome for employees (faculty) to control product quality and quantity. Indeed, a compulsion may exist to want to run the college or university as if it were a for-profit corporation. Faculty and deans generally reject the uncritical application of the corporate model to education, however, arguing that the academy is not a business where knowledge or management authority can be centralized. Although a place should be kept for the market, the market should be kept in its place.

The capital costs of entry into the higher education market have been substantially reduced for online institutions, however. Although the initial development costs for multimedia courses can be high—60 percent of the total cost of an online course over its first five years is for development—content can increasingly be sourced externally (Bates, 2000). Whereas a professor taught a small class at a direct and indirect cost of some $300 per hour, online course delivery has a marginal cost of about three cents per hour. Even when online tutoring by adjunct faculty is added, the cost is approximately $30 per hour. In sum, instructional technology can minimize capital and operating costs while maximizing geographical reach.

The governance and funding of higher education have been deeply rooted in the philosophy that college teaching is labor intensive. It is argued that the traditional model of liberal education associated with such an approach fosters both learning and leadership. In 2000, an estimated 40 percent of Fortune 500 chief executives graduated from a liberal arts college or received a degree with a liberal arts major. As "affinity beings," students enjoy learning among other students in a context of sustained social interaction. Their thoughts and ideas are validated by face-to-face discussion (Durden, 2001). Yet e-learning may be not only a vital tool for the delivery of workplace training and adult continuing education but also a useful supplement to liberal education (National Association of College and University Business Officers, 1997). If chat rooms and instant messaging techniques cannot yet mirror small-group seminars effectively, instructional technologies continue to evolve. The inherent advantages of traditional liberal arts education remain the values added for eighteen- to twenty-four-year-old undergraduates in residential environments and the intensive socialization inherent in learning how to learn as well as to think critically.

E-Learning: Policy Issues and Impact

E-learning has moved the cost of education toward the design side. Educational specialists, who design course structure and focus on the delivery method rather than the actual content, are becoming more and more common. Once a course has been designed and delivered to a few students, in principle it can be duplicated very cost-effectively to hundreds, even thousands, of other learners. If the course content belongs to the individual faculty member as his or her intellectual property (a position held by the American Association of University Professors) but the design and delivery belong to the university, who actually owns the course? Many universities consider distance courses their property, created by their employees as work for hire. An industry-wide agreement that the intellectual copyright on course materials is vested in the employing institution rather than the faculty member is likely to retard the development of online education.

The central issue that any institution wishing to develop e-learning programs must examine is its intellectual property policy. An effective online distance education policy establishes clear patent, copyright, and software policy statements and may also involve the use of logos, trademarks, or other institutional symbols such as the campus mascot. Intellectual property rights must establish ownership of the distance education course. What are the institutional and faculty rights and responsibilities after the course is created and offered online? In fact, these issues should be settled well before the course is online.

Most universities find that distance learning intellectual property rights cannot be organized into a single statement. For instance, faculty may want to argue that distance education course material should be covered by the university's copyright policy, whereas the financial officer may want to focus on the cost to the institution and argue that such material is covered by the patent policy. Meanwhile, small colleges may not even have such copyright or patent policies in place.

One approach is to offer copyright protection to the creators of a course while dividing ownership of the course into content and design (Chambers, 1999). Professors continue to control the actual content. If a faculty member leaves the university or the course is sold to another institution, the faculty member who generated the content maintains control, receiving royalties and continuing to manage the course's content. This approach encourages faculty and staff to contribute to online course development, while the instructional design remains the property of the institution where the course was created. By 2001, such a policy had been adopted by a number of institutions, including the University of Vermont (Carnevale, 2001).

The underlying dilemma is by no means fully resolved, however. Although this ownership policy is faculty friendly, many questions remain to be answered. Under our current philosophy, colleges and universities operate for the common good. Public and private support is based on the perception that colleges and universities deserve financial support as education is beneficial to everyone. If an institution's activities are seen as property that can be sold and has real value or commercial worth, then the public's perception of the university's mission may be compromised (Berube, 1996). Stakeholders may question the mission of higher education, which will inevitably raise questions about the level of support to be provided.

Can college and university governance move toward more effective governance systems, taking the e-learning environment fully into account? Shared governance is not readily associated with entrepreneurship, rapid decision making, timely market differentiation, and effective management of distribution channels. At risk is a system that has accomplished much, not through private gain or government regulation but through governance structures committed to the higher common good, in principle and usually in practice. Traditionally, student learning and the public interest have been core values in the organizational cultures of every college and university, and although these objectives have not always been clearly spelled out in mission and vision statements, they have usually been at least implicit. By contrast, the pursuit of private institutional and individual gain has become one of the key goals of twenty-first-century higher education.

An underlying premise has been that public and private interests in higher education can readily collaborate to advance the public purpose, exemplified by customized research undertaken by public research universities and subsidized by private businesses, and by customized worker training at community colleges and other institutions. Meanwhile, for-profit ventures have been increasingly spawned from public universities and nonprofit educational institutions, with the unintended result that the viability of private alternatives might provide a rationale for diminishing public investment in higher education as the perceived public good diminishes (Longanecker, 2001). This possibility presents one of the fundamental challenges of university governance in the twenty-first century.

E-learning continues to exemplify this challenge. Perhaps one indicator as to just how important such education is to higher education and to university governance is the number of related journal articles now available. For instance, a series of articles appeared in *Trusteeship* in November/December 2000,

Change in September/October 2000, and *Academe* in May/June 2001. The headline on the cover of *Academe* is instructive: "In It Together—Faculty, Administrators, and Shared Governance." Meanwhile, the cover of *Change* proclaimed "E-Learning—The Tradeoff between Richness and Reach." It remains the case that distance education can also facilitate the creation of diploma mills, especially when unaccredited. This concern led the Louisiana board of regents to refuse to renew the operating licenses of Bienville, Columbus, Glenford, and Lacrosse Universities on October 1, 2002 (Foster, 2002).

What will the future hold for higher education? Will a kind of cooperative model emerge, or will colleges and universities become more like health maintenance organizations? Will faculty become entrepreneurs and superstars, enjoying an international demand for their services, or find themselves mostly relegated to work similar to that of graduate teaching assistants? None of these alternatives are attractive to faculty or senior administrators, as any would fundamentally change the role of faculty in higher education. Questions of academic freedom and quality would be raised, perhaps with serious consequences for public perceptions of higher education. A more agreeable approach conceivably can be found somewhere in between if professors and their institutions share ownership and governance of e-learning programs and courses, much as they do of patented research.

Resource Allocation
and Governance

E VERY UNIVERSITY AND COLLEGE governance system must come to grips with resource allocation. In other words, it must address the recurrent questions of who receives what, when, why, and how, in an effective and equitable manner.

Responsibility-Centered Management

Nowhere does the perception of shared governance have more potential for conflict than in the area of budget and finances (Griffin, 1993). Who is responsible for what and why? We have discussed the concept of the single-system image of a university that can transform its administration. This vision and commitment may also be required in an area that cuts across institutional structures and processes in colleges and universities despite the reported evidence that some administrators tend to view decentralized budgeting and effective governance as insignificantly related. Indeed, the higher education environment strongly suggests the need to manage the significant improvement of revenue and reduction of expenses in an inclusive manner that contributes effectively to institutional missions.

Many universities have found that the further integration of strategic planning and budgeting is well served by the introduction of a modified responsibility management system. Such an approach may not only significantly contribute to Continuous Quality Improvement in university communities but also allow for the formulation of proactive stances, especially with regard to public education performance-funding initiatives, which various legislatures have adopted. By 1997, the states where the practice of performance-based funding was most advanced included New York, Wisconsin, Texas, South Carolina, Colorado, and Missouri. All but a handful of U.S. states appear likely to implement such models in the near future (*Assessment Update,* 1997). In fact, responsibility-centered management (RCM) may be viewed as the most dynamic, decentralized, and efficient method of performance-based program budgeting. But how does RCM change the perceptions of shared governance?

Performance-Based Program Budgeting: The Basic Questions

This topic is challenging, as consensus concerning the utility of specific performance indicators has yet to be achieved. Although extensive sets of competing measuring rods continue to proliferate across the states, these units of measurements essentially encapsulate the following basic questions (Keller, 1996):

- How well are admitted students prepared for university-level learning?
- What happens to students after they enroll? How many graduate? What fields do they enter?
- How much do university graduates know? What can they do as a result of their undergraduate studies?
- What special programs are in place to assist minorities and immigrant students?
- Are publicly supported (or assisted) universities assisting with the special economic needs of their states in areas such as technology, engineering, health care, teaching, and business? If so, how and how well?
- How efficiently are public universities using their physical facilities and allocating their financial resources?
- How productive is the faculty? How much teaching do they really do, and how well do they teach? Does the array of courses offered make sense?

A key point is that performance assessment is effectively internalized when the strategic planning and management processes of a university encapsulate

Continuous Quality Improvement while anticipating and meeting the needs of constituents. The main principles of responsibility-centered management are summarily reviewed so as to provide a prism through which to view reported expenditures as well as the single most efficient and effective method of linking the strategic planning and budgetary processes.

Benchmark Institution Practices
This method was pioneered by a number of research and doctoral institutions and is being implemented by more and more universities today, across the gamut of baccalaureate, comprehensive, and research institutions.

The RCM model makes five key assumptions:

- Some programs are inherently more expensive than others and require more investment resources than they can be expected to generate.
- Opportunities for income from sponsored research and private giving vary among colleges and schools.
- "Investor" colleges are expected to contribute up to 50 percent of net resources to the central administration annually.
- Colleges' performance will be analyzed carefully each year to determine return on investment.
- Capital investment dollars will be generated based on a formula and available each year, using the cash from incremental faculty positions.

Principles of Responsibility-Centered Management
Responsibility-centered management, initially known as responsibility-centered budgeting, was pioneered at the University of Pennsylvania, the University of Southern California, and a number of other independent universities during the late 1970s, and at Indiana University in the early 1980s. Other major universities with experience in RCM include Illinois, Michigan, Minnesota, and Penn State.

RCM provides the single most effective method available for linking unit budgets and academic priorities. It has three underlying principles:

1. All costs and income attributable to each academic or administrative profit center should be assigned to that unit;

2. Appropriate incentives should exist for each unit to increase income and reduce costs continuously, so as to further agreed university-wide strategy;

3. All the costs of support units or cost centers, such as libraries or student counseling, should be allocated to particular profit centers (Whalen, 1991).

In relatively small institutions, centralized resource allocation may be practicable, if not necessarily desirable, as both direct and indirect costs and revenue flows can be ascertained with relative ease. As an institution moves up the enrollment and operating budget scale, however, the case for a decentralized system of decision making and resource allocation is increasingly strong, because the links between costs, performance, and revenues become more and more complex. For example, the impact of unit operating costs on the level of resources devoted to indirect costs tends to become more difficult to isolate. At a smaller private university, however, the case is not as compelling.

Responsibility-centered management is intended to provide incentives for colleges, schools, and departments to undertake excellent teaching, research, and service, thus increasing potential income generated while providing information that can lead to significant new efficiencies in university structure and processes (Meyers, 1994). Accountability and authority are decentralized, and faculty involvement in planning and budgeting is increased, allowing for greater flexibility. Under such a bottom-up system of decision making, it becomes clear which units are subsidized and to what extent, thus inviting—indeed requiring—justification.

The ten basic concepts of responsibility-centered management are applicable in any organization, whether public or private, non-profit or for-profit:

1. Operating decisions are likely to be better the closer they are to the point of implementation.

2. A clearly explained balance between decentralization and centralization is desirable in the interests of increased unit efficiency.

3. The optimal level of decentralization is directly related to organizational size and complexity.

4. Full information concerning benefits and consequences increases the probability of accurate decision making.
5. Responsibility for resource management should be commensurate with related authority.
6. Excellent managerial performance should be automatically recognized and rewarded.
7. Relatively stable internal environments where performance expectations do not change arbitrarily facilitate good planning and performance.
8. The interrelationship of the parts of the community to the whole institution should be explicitly reflected in resource allocation.
9. Senior management should determine the level of services required for the collective benefit of the institution and retain sufficient resources to ensure that such services are consistently funded.
10. Unit and individual managerial performance is best evaluated in the context of a comprehensive, clearly articulated, and accepted multiyear strategic plan.

In sum, a responsibility center receives the income generated by its activities while incurring all costs, direct and indirect, associated with such activities. Meanwhile, support units or cost centers receive income in the form of charges to academic units for services rendered as well as centrally allocated revenues, as necessary, based on the university's strategic priorities while incurring all costs related to service delivery.

At the end of the budget year, both positive and negative balances are carried forward as contributions toward or obligations against future resources. RCM is designed to make the budget process responsive to academic priorities and requires an information-rich environment. Thus, it is essential for the university's human resources, academic, financial, and student affairs databases to be fully integrated and for information to be broadly available to all employees with implementation responsibilities, as advocated by the principles of "open-book management." Under open-book management, each employee sees and learns to track his institution's financial data and to understand the contribution of his own job to these results while developing a sense of an individual stake in institutional success (Case, 1995).

Caveats and Adjustments
to Responsibility-Centered Management

It is worth emphasizing that RCM is not presented as a panacea. Instead, such a system needs to be adjusted to meet the strategic imperatives and historical idiosyncrasies of each organization that adopts it. The problems encountered with RCM may be grouped in four categories. First is the charge that collegiality is reduced, because cooperation between colleges and schools is diminished. This situation is often clearest where multidisciplinary projects or programs are concerned. The flip side of this concern is that internal competition is intensified to offer more courses and to recruit or retain students by steps that might include grade inflation. Further, the attribution of revenue from instructional activities may bring into focus the issue of which academic center should be teaching what courses.

Second is the potential to encourage extreme measures of cost control and revenue enhancement, including expanded use of temporary faculty, and a proliferation of fees. Third, noninstructional units, or cost centers, may be at the mercy of the central administration for the bulk of their resources, even as profit centers complain that they have insufficient control over the management and mission of support units. Fourth, given that the level of discretionary funding available to the central administration tends to be significantly reduced, the danger arises that unprofitable strategic priorities might be underfunded. Before implementing RCM, university leaders and managers should explore such issues in detail.

In the course of implementing RCM, the major challenges arise more from human attitudes and the weight of institutional tradition than from technical issues, although the installation of appropriate budget software, such as SAP or PeopleSoft, is required for the efficient assignment of cost and revenue centers. An initial step is to decide on an appropriate level of unit subvention to the central administration so as to fund university-wide strategic priorities. Each unit then makes its case for additional funding, in this context. As an example, the University of Southern California taxes each college or school 20 percent of its student fee and indirect cost recovery income, then combines the result with other revenue sources, including interest from unrestricted accounts. The redistribution of this revenue pool across the university is driven by USC's long-term strategic objectives.

In public universities, legislative or governing board priorities may be more readily incorporated into the planning process, thus effectively internalizing performance funding. It is then relatively easy to identify profit and cost centers, attribute income, and allocate indirect costs to each center and direct charges to support unit services. The next step is to provide complete statements of account in this format to all administrators with related responsibilities. The task of explaining RCM principles clearly and responding to all articulated concerns satisfactorily is typically much more demanding. It may therefore be important to establish a respected and representative steering committee, whose charge is to identify best practices and build support from the campus community early in the implementation process.

The more technical concerns mentioned above may be addressed by implementing measures such as the identification of a discretionary fund intended to leverage strategic priorities. It is also possible to expand incentives to support units by permitting them to retain access to a significant percentage of year-end balances for approved expenditures in future years, while implementing regularly applied performance measures for such cost centers. At a more general level, the president or chancellor might use every opportunity to foster a climate of collegiality and cooperation across the university community.

In spring 1996, the National Association of College and University Business Officers conducted a two-part survey regarding the use and effectiveness of RCM on university campuses. NACUBO sent the first survey to 600 member institutions and followed up with a more detailed survey, sent to institutions using "institutional financial management systems having decentralized financial accountability for both revenues and expenses, as well as incentives for all unit leaders to achieve positive financial performance."

A total of 235 higher education institutions responded, 68 percent public and 32 percent private (West, Seidata, di Mattia, and Whalen, 1997). The main findings of these surveys were that:

1. Relatively small as well as large colleges and universities had found RCM useful;

2. Fewer public than independent universities had implemented RCM systems;

3. State universities appeared to be less aware of the concept than their private counterparts; and

4. Only one institution chose to partially move away from RCM after implementation as a result of a change in management philosophy.

The majority of implementing universities and colleges cited very successful results. At the same time, the results of these surveys reinforce the message that RCM can be successful only when an institution has clear academic priorities and commits itself to these priorities with its budget.

These NACUBO surveys also suggested four areas of concern: organizational structure, financial information for decision making, external interference, and efforts to beat the system. In an RCM environment, the absolute as well as relative size of academic units can become an issue. For example, a small college of health may be much more susceptible to swings in enrollment, income, and staffing than a very large school of medicine or college of business administration, while the latter may be unable to respond quickly to environmental changes.

In turn, traditional accountability and program review reports are designed to provide information to academic affairs and to the president's office while complying with the requirements of state and federal agencies and accrediting agencies. But RCM systems also require units to account for indirect as well as direct costs. Revenues and expenditures must be attributed to centers. Current management information must be provided to all units in a decentralized manner. At the University of North Florida, for example, an institutional research office has had to expend much effort to reorganize its data reporting significantly so as to meet program review requirements, even though the lack of "carry-forward" authority from the state and the relatively small budget have limited the immediate appeal of RCM. Meanwhile, the inability of this public institution to retain its year-end balances and the potential for earned income to replace appropriated funds illustrate how governance structure can constrain university financial management. Other state regulations and administrative requirements such as central approval of purchases and the need to use a particular accounting system can also impede the implementation of RCM.

The experience of NACUBO survey respondents suggests that seven common factors underlie successful implementation of RCM:

- Support from senior university executives and the governing board;
- Communication of projected benefits and time for discussion of outcomes;
- An explicit link between RCM and clearly articulated institutional missions and goals;
- The establishment of milestones and the measurement of progress toward them;
- Continued communication and a willingness to correct emerging problems;
- Managed expectations oriented toward the medium to long term;
- Requisites for successful institutional transformation, including the need to adjust some aspects of organizational culture while maintaining or strengthening others.

RCM can readily facilitate the enhancement of shared governance, as the unit leader's responsibilities and authority are clearly established. Operational decisions and implementation are closely linked. Managerial performance can be more effectively evaluated. Yet RCM can encourage dysfunctional internal competition and focus attention on profit, even at the expense of the core educational mission of a college or university. This is the point where effective institutional leadership and management become vital.

A Revised Model of Governance Structure in the Twenty-First-Century University

W E HAVE DEFINED UNIVERSITY governance as the structure and process of authoritative decision making across stakeholder-significant issues. Governance may be further interpreted as a decision-making arena contoured by culture, history, and geography within which presidents, faculty, senior administrators, trustees, state legislators, governors, and other interested participants recurrently address core issues such as leadership, strategic direction, institutional transformation, educational technology, teaching and learning processes, overall resource allocation, strategic priorities and outcomes, and accountability.

We also identified three core governance-related issues for discussion: teaching and learning, information technology and distance education, and resource allocation and accountability. We reviewed the many current challenges to university governance structures, considered the constraints and opportunities created by organizational culture, and explored the divergences between the perspectives and expectations among core university community participants apart from students—and faculty, senior administrators and presidents, and trustees.

Interdependent stakeholders constitute the formal participants in university governance structures. Issues such as academic freedom, institutional accountability, quality, peer review, authority and responsibility, information flows, access, participation, and budget allocations determine the agenda. Each participant's daily decisions and actions are informed by a set of specific values, beliefs, hopes, and fears, and the eventual results are conditioned by the organizational context. Different emphases are placed on disciplinary groups, chains of command, political relationships, social needs, and competitive markets. Any immediate decision context, however, may be subject to recurrent intersubjective verification. It cannot be assumed, for instance, that an actionable consensus exists as to whether eddying currents or rapids lie ahead for a given college or university. Leaders are paid to look around the bend and under surface effects while noting situational shades of gray and identifying actual or potential sources of significant misunderstanding such as the requisites for effective governance in the twenty-first-century university.

George Winston (1997) rhetorically asks why a college can't be more like a firm. The answer is both deceptively simple and complex. A higher education institution typically pursues multiple goals in its creation of an effective learning environment: programs and curricula of demonstrably high quality; the socialization and creation of graduates able to engage in critical thinking, teamwork, and continuous learning; the facilitation and production of pure and applied research; community service, which might include workforce training; excellent public relations; building and campus maintenance; and technology transfer and revenue generation to exist and thrive. Such an institution seeks to simultaneously satisfy a broad range of stakeholders. In contrast, a firm is expected to focus on profit generation and shareholder value. University and college presidents, on the other hand, spend increasing amounts of time raising funds, even in times of limited price inflation, as financial aid and equipment costs multiply, competition for excellent students and faculty members intensifies, and deferred maintenance and construction costs mount. At the same time, expanding competition from for-profit training and educational institutions and the need to increase entrepreneurial activities at home and abroad imply an increasing focus on cost control and profit generation, at least potentially at the expense of other university or college goals.

The model shown in Figure 4 owes a great deal to the work of Robert Birnbaum and others; it places the attitudes, values, and expectations of internal and external stakeholders at the center. Breakpoint change impulses interpreted and acted upon by faculty, administrators, students, trustees, and presidents continually traverse this open system. Some responses may be positive, expressed in terms of rules, policies, and budgets that contribute to systemic survival and vitality; others may exemplify negative entropy.

FIGURE 4
Twenty-first Century University Governance Structure

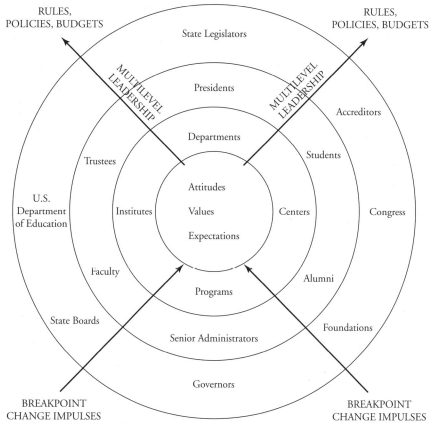

In this model, other inputs, processes, outputs, and outcomes are actually all mediated by the independent variables represented by stakeholders' attitudes, values, and expectations. Structures such as departments, institutes, and centers, policies of federal and state governments, legislative decisions, the goals of relevant foundations, and the criteria applied by regional accrediting associations remain important. But they are not necessarily determining factors. Let us imagine an institution where the president, senior administrators, faculty, trustees, students, and alumni often function as leaders at several levels, sharing a mostly consensual understanding of the policy environment and working together to implement agreed-upon goals, at least much of the time. In such a case, breakpoint change impulses—as well as more routine challenges—might sometimes cause serious concern. But institutional outputs, and eventually outcomes, would usually be likely to illuminate the meaning of the proverbial question Today is the tomorrow you were worried about yesterday; was it worth it?

Shared governance, as traditionally defined, is clearly obsolescent and requires reinterpretation in an increasingly dynamic and global higher education market. Never before have so many kinds of university stakeholders been more conscious of the outputs and perceived outcomes of institutional decisions or more willing to articulate their concerns, sometimes stridently. Put simply, not simplistically, governance must be shared among all major stakeholders, not just faculty, students, administrators, and trustees, on the basis of mutual respect and open communication. For example, advisory, consultative, and decision-making committees must be clearly distinguished, and each should have specific terms of reference and unambiguous sunset provisions. A university must function effectively as a community, capable of generating value for most members, even though it may emphasize varied parts of the elephant at particular times. To thrive, university communities will need to learn to generate and use resources in flexible, responsive, and imaginative ways based on current market intelligence. The delegation of management responsibility to the level closest to the immediate consequences of decisions taken is a critical component of such an orientation. It implies a need for authentic leadership, the effective use of information technology, and the application of various frames of reference at multiple institutional levels. In turn, such leadership requires the development of a personal vision based on individual identity and goals and a continuously perceived link between organizational and personal needs.

At the outset, we posed a number of fundamental questions, which were answered in subsequent chapters. How are governance systems structured and the interplay between organizational culture, institutional mission, and university governance structure best defined? What exactly is the difference between managing universities in a businesslike manner and treating a university like a business? What distinction needs to be made between education and training? If it is widely agreed that university governance structures require significant adjustment, how is it to be done? In exactly what ways, what sequence, and by whom? What kinds of institutional leadership will best address the multiple challenges that have been identified and discussed? What are the specific policy directions that leaders seeking to shape the university of the twenty-first century must take into account, given the nature of the higher education environment?

As higher education institutions continue to evolve in a perpetually changing environment, it is indeed probable that significant rationalization will occur, leaving several hundred community colleges, small liberal arts colleges, large research universities, and well-funded and -branded e-learning institutions to provide most education and training in America. Both faculty tenure and sovereignty over the curriculum are likely to diminish, except, perhaps, in selected liberal arts colleges and research universities. In a return to the fourth century B.C., when Socrates, Plato, and Solon led groups of followers in problem-based discussion and learning, some faculty entrepreneurs may find a formal university appointment superfluous, while many others might well assume the roles of learning experience designers, facilitators, and mentors. As educational technologies evolve, many more colleges and universities will need to choose whether to emphasize the development or the delivery of academic content. Effective university leadership and strategic management will remain essential for decision making, implementation, and evaluation, and for harnessing appropriate resources strategically in a complex environment.

What should presidents, trustees, and faculty leaders carry away from this extended exploration of attitudes in the academy, challenges to governance structures, competing expectations, and significant environmental trends inside and outside academic institutions? To paraphrase Kahlil Gibran, the obvious is sometimes overlooked until it is simply stated. In essence, universities and colleges are ordered sociopolitical and socioeconomic communities of students, teachers, scholars, and leaders. There is no substitute for community dialogue that includes trustees, administrators, faculty, and students about the relationship between teaching, research, and governance structure. Yet leaders must also be prepared to find that such dialogue might reveal new differences in attitudes and values that might not have been previously anticipated but need to be addressed. In such cases, it may be possible to work patiently within identified collegial networks and eventually to fold multiple perspectives together while creating rolling coalitions for change by developing an increasingly shared vision of the future.

Similarly, leaders have a tendency to pay insufficient attention to at least some of the core elements of institutional culture such as mission, historical traditions, values, community expectations, and other distinctive characteristics, perhaps because culture remains a rather amorphous concept. Yet the culture of a college or university can be productively viewed as a potential competitive advantage, one that might need to be actualized. In the course of drawing upon the resources represented by culture for the purposes of mission fulfillment, the broccoli floret remains a helpful analogy. Trust must become a fractal, part of each community member's basic belief system, if culture is to make more than a rhetorical difference. Indeed, significant institutional transformation cannot occur without prior cultural change that facilitates realigned missions and governance structures.

In turn, student and faculty demand and the rapid succession of increasingly powerful and expensive hardware and software configurations have driven the expansion of information technology across our campuses. But information technology can also enhance communication between faculty and students, between administrators and faculty, between trustees and administrators, and between faculty and trustees. Such technology can also facilitate decentralization of the budgetary process, distributed responsibility and authority, and more effectively shared governance. New approaches to university leadership and management are essential if effective information technology strategies are to be implemented.

Much more work on the subject of governance is naturally warranted. More of the vast related literature merits discussion and analysis. Additional research might include case studies and stratified focus groups regarding the nature and implications of institutional culture, the role of decentralized budgeting schemes in university decision making, and the strategies that can best encourage positive long-term change, given specific environmental challenges. The present study suggests means by which university leaders can improve the establishment of priorities while establishing or refining management systems that truly clarify roles, balance collaboration with decision making, and link authority to responsibility.

Effective university leadership requires purpose, energy, and enthusiasm. It implies a series of intentional choices for oneself and one's institution.

The university of the twenty-first century is already evolving before our eyes. Such universities are both local, rooted in their regional communities, and global in the scope of their networks of intellectual contact. They consist of communities of scholars, learners, leaders, managers, and other significant stakeholders. The twenty-first-century university is much more an intellectual space, underpinned by instructional technologies, values, ideas, revenue flows, and sociopolitical legitimacy, than a physical space with a specific set of buildings—although well-landscaped campuses will continue to contribute to institutional branding for the purposes of defined target audiences. In any case, institutional and individual branding, where desirable deliverables are promoted, generated, evaluated, and enhanced, over time will remain essential. Some universities will identify competitive niches and continually reinvent themselves to meet the changing needs of their constituents. Many others will find themselves considering choices that include repeated budgetary crises and cuts, and efforts at transformation that follow rather than anticipate environmental change, merger, and closure. What is required is university governance that, in structure and process, encourages and facilitates positive, proactive, and continuous institutional transformation together with relationship-building strategies focused on stakeholders as well as markets and sustained revenue generation.

Appendix A: Public and Private University Enrollments, 1998

	Public	Private
Australia	100.0%	—
Austria	97.4	2.6%
Brazil	41.1	59.9
Canada	100.0	—
Czech Republic	100.0	—
France	91.0	9.0
Germany	100.0	—
Hungary	88.2	11.8
Indonesia	29.7	70.3
Ireland	94.1	5.9
Japan	26.1	73.9
Malaysia	92.9	7.1
New Zealand	99.3	0.7
Philippines	24.8	75.2
South Korea	24.3	75.7
Spain	89.5	10.5
Sri Lanka	100.0	—
Thailand	85.8	14.2
Turkey	98.3	1.7
United States	68.9	31.1

Note: The Organization for Economic Cooperation and Development classifies educational institutions as public or private according to whether a public agency or private entity has the ultimate power to make decisions concerning the institution's affairs. The extent to which an institution receives funds from public or private sources does not determine the classification status of the institution.

Source: OECD Education Database, 2000.

Appendix B: Survey of University Governance

Instructions: Please assess the relative importance of each point raised, as well as your agreement or disagreement, respectively, on scales of 1 to 5 (with 5 representing either substantial significance or complete concordance). It would be much appreciated if your responses were returned by April 10, 1998.

Scale Definition:

Importance:

0 = Doesn't Apply; 1 = Insignificant; 2 = Somewhat Insignificant; 3 = Neutral; 4 = Significant; 5 = Very Significant

Agreement:

0 = Doesn't Apply; 1 = Strongly Disagree; 2 = Disagree; 3 = Neutral; 4 = Agree; 5 = Strongly Agree

1 Current pressures for restructuring have significantly impacted our university within the last 5 years.

Importance Level _____   Agreement Level _____

2 Our university is becoming less hierarchical than it was.

Importance Level _____   Agreement Level _____

3 Our university is becoming more inclined toward shared governance than it was.

Importance Level _____   Agreement Level _____

4 Our present governance structure matches authority with accountability.

Importance Level _____   Agreement Level _____

5 Our current governance structure is hindered by our university's organizational culture.

Importance Level _____ Agreement Level _____

6 Newly developed management information systems have made much more information available to all participants in governance at our university than was possible before.

Importance Level_____ Agreement Level _____

7 In response to the increasing pressures to make decisions quickly, we are moving toward growing decentralization in governance.

Importance Level _____ Agreement Level _____

8 At our university, we have been able to define the areas of governance where faculty members rather than administrators should have primary roles. (Please list these areas on the reverse side.)

Importance Level _____ Agreement Level _____

9 Our current university governance system is not affected by the presence of a faculty union.

Importance Level _____ Agreement Level _____

10 At our university, governance is focused on means of enhancing learning and teaching.

Importance Level _____ Agreement Level _____

11 A decentralized budgetary system, such as responsibility-centered management, has strengthened (or would strengthen) governance at our university.

Importance Level _____ Agreement Level _____

12 In university state system governance, it is generally desirable to increase system- rather than institution-level economies of scope and scale and/or to foster joint ventures between members.

Importance Level _____ Agreement Level_____

Appendix C: Organizational Culture and Governance

	Faculty			Administrators		
	B	C	D/R	B	C	D/R
"Our current governance structure is underpinned by my university's organizational culture."						
Organizational Culture Significance	63%	65%	82%	57%	68%	79%
Organizational Culture Insignificance	9%	8%	4%	19%	15%	6%
Agree/Strongly Agree	47%	50%	67%	47%	61%	67%
Disagree/Strongly Disagree	30%	29%	15%	33%	26%	19%

Notes: B = baccalaureate; C = comprehensive; D/R = doctoral/research. Responses from faculty and administrators are compared by level of significance ascribed to organizational culture and by agreement or disagreement with the selected statement.

References

Altbach, P. G. (2002, Fall). Farewell to the common good: Knowledge and education as international commodities. *International Education,* pp. 13–17.

American Association of University Professors. (1968). *Statement on government of colleges and universities.* [http://www.aaup.org/govern.htm].

American Association of University Professors. (1994, July–August). Report on the relationship of faculty governance to academic freedom. *Academe.*

Argyris, C. (1991). Teaching smart people how to learn. *Harvard Business Review,* 31.

Armstrong, L. (2000). An academic leader's perspective on a disruptive product. *Change, 32*(6).

Assessment Update: Progress, Trends, and Practices in Higher Education. (1997, January–February). *9*(1).

Association of Governing Boards of Universities and Colleges. (1998). *Bridging the gap between state government and public higher education.* Washington, DC: Association of Governing Boards of Universities and Colleges.

Association of Governing Boards of Universities and Colleges. (1999). *AGB statement on institutional governance.* Washington, DC: Association of Governing Boards of Universities and Colleges. [http://www.agb.org/governance.cfm].

Astin, A. W. (1993). *Higher education and the concept of community.* Urbana: University of Illinois.

Astin, A. W., and Associates. (2001). *The theory and practice of institutional transformation in higher education.* Los Angeles: Higher Education Research Institute, University of California, Los Angeles.

Auden, W. H. (1965). *About the house.* New York: Random House.

Baez, B., and Centra, J. A. (1995). *Tenure, promotion and reappointment: Legal and administrative implications.* ASHE-ERIC Higher Education Report, no. 1. Washington, DC: School of Education and Human Development, George Washington University.

Baldridge, J. V., Curtis, D. V., Ecker, G. P., and Riley, G. L. (1986). Alternative models of governance in higher education. In M. W. Peterson (Ed.), *ASHE reader on organization and governance in higher education.* Lexington, MA: Ginn Press.

Barak, R., and Sweeney, J. (1995). *Academic program review in planning, budgeting, and assessment.* In R. Barak and L. A. Mets (Eds.), *Using academic program review.* New Directions for Institutional Research, no. 86. San Francisco: Jossey-Bass.

Barrow, C. W. (1990). *Universities and the capitalist state: Corporate liberalism and the reconstruction of American higher education, 1894–1928.* Madison: University of Wisconsin Press.

Basinger, J. (1999a, August 13). In evaluating the college president, governing boards assert more authority. *Chronicle of Higher Education.*

Basinger, J. (1999b, June 22). University of South Alabama trustees sue to dissolve foundation. *Chronicle of Higher Education.*

Basinger, J. (2001, August 10). Peer review. *Chronicle of Higher Education.*

Bates, A. W. (2000). *Managing technological change.* San Francisco: Jossey-Bass.

Baucus, M., and Near, J. (1991). Can illegal corporate behavior be predicted? An event history analysis. *Academy of Management Journal, 34*(1), 15–34.

Benjamin, R., and Carroll, S. (1998). The implications of the changed environment for governance in higher education. In W. Tierney (Ed.), *The responsive university* (pp. 92–119). Baltimore: Johns Hopkins University Press.

Bennis, W., and Nanus, B. (1985). *Leaders: New strategies for taking charge.* New York: Harper & Row.

Bennis, W., Spreitzer, G. M., and Cummings, T. G. [Eds.] (2001). *The future of leadership: Today's top leadership thinkers speak to tomorrow's leaders.* San Francisco: Jossey-Bass.

Berube, M. (1996). Public perceptions of universities and faculty. *Academe, 82*(4).

Bess, J. L. (1992). Collegiality: Toward a clarification of meaning and function. In J. C. Smart (Ed.), *Higher education: Handbook of theory and research* (Vol. 3). Edison, NJ: Agathon Press.

Biggs, J. (1996). Assessing learning quality: Reconciling institutional, staff and educational demands. *Assessment and Evaluation in Higher Education, 21*(1).

Biggs, J. (1999). *Teaching for quality learning at university.* Buckingham, Eng., and Philadelphia: Society for Research into Higher Education and Open University Press.

Birnbaum, R. (1988). *How colleges work: The cybernetics of academic organization and leadership.* San Francisco: Jossey-Bass.

Birnbaum R. (1989). The latent organizational functions of the academic senate: Why senates do not work but will not go away. *Journal of Higher Education, 60*(4).

Birnbaum, R. (1990). *Will you love me in December as you do in May? Why experienced college presidents lose faculty support.* Paper presented at the Annual Meeting of the Association for the Study of Higher Education, November 1–4, Portland, OR.

Birnbaum, R. [Ed.] (1991). *Faculty in governance: The role of senates and joint committees in academic decision making.* New Directions for Higher Education, no. 75. San Francisco: Jossey-Bass.

Birnbaum, R. (1992). *How academic leadership works: Understanding success and failure in the college presidency.* San Francisco: Jossey-Bass.

Blimling, G. S., and Whitt, E. J. (1999). *Good practice in student affairs: Principles to foster student learning.* San Francisco: Jossey-Bass.

Bolman, L. G., and Deal, T. E. (1997). *Reframing organizations: Artistry, choice, and leadership*. San Francisco: Jossey-Bass.

Bowen, R. (2001, June 22). The new battle between political and academic cultures. *Chronicle of Higher Education*.

Bowie, N. E. (1994). *University-business partnerships: An assessment*. Lanham, MD: Rowman & Littlefield.

Boyer, E. L. (1990). *Scholarship reconsidered: Priorities of the professoriate*. Princeton, NJ: Carnegie Foundation for the Advancement of Teaching.

Braithwaite, J. (1989). *Crime, shame and reintegration*. New York: Cambridge University Press.

Bransten, L. (2001, March 12). Something ventured. *Wall Street Journal*.

Breslin, R. D. (2000, November 10). Lessons from the presidential trenches. *Chronicle of Higher Education*, A56.

Bronfenbrenner, K., and Juravich, T. (2001, Jan. 19). Universities should cease hostilities with unions. *Chronicle of Higher Education*.

Brown, M. (1991). Cosmopolitans as heralds of a vitalized faculty role. *Academe, 77*(5).

Brown, S., and Knight, P. (1994). *Assessing learners in higher education*. London, Eng.: Kogan Page.

Brown, W. O., Jr. (2001). Faculty participation in university governance and the effects on university performance. *Journal of Economic Behavior & Organization, 44*(2), 129.

Brownstein, A. (2001, April 19). After sounding warning on enrollment, president of all-female Hollins University resigns. *Chronicle of Higher Education*.

Brubacher, J. S., and Rudy, W. (1997). *Higher education in transition: A history of American colleges and universities*. New Brunswick, NJ: Transaction Publishers.

Building and leading successful learning communities. (2000, December). *Dean and Provost, 2*(4), 3–4.

Burke, J. C. (1997). *Performance-funding indicators: Concerns, values and models for two- and four-year colleges and universities*. Albany: Rockefeller Institute, State University of New York.

Burke, J. C., and Serban, A. M. (1998). *Current status and future prospects of performance funding and performance budgeting for public higher education: The second survey*. Albany: Rockefeller Institute, State University of New York.

Burnside, R. M. (2001, July–August). E-learning for adults: Who has the goods? *Commentary*.

Buttrick, W. (1922, August). The general education board. *School and Society, 16,* 17–19.

Callan, P. M., Doyle, W., and Finney, J. E. (2001). Evaluating state higher education performance: Measuring Up 2000. *Change, 33*(2).

Carnegie Commission on Higher Education (1973). *Governance of higher education*. New York: McGraw Hill.

Carnegie Foundation for the Advancement of Teaching (1982). *The control of the campus: A report on the governance of higher education*. Carnegie: Washington, DC.

Carnevale, D. (2000, September 21). Accrediting bodies consider new standards for distance-education programs. *Chronicle of Higher Education*.

Carnevale, D. (2001, May 21). U. of Vermont considers intellectual-property policy said to foster distance education. *Chronicle of Higher Education*.

Case, J. (1995). *Open book management: The coming business revolution.* New York: Harper Business.

Chait, R. (1995). *The new activism of corporate boards and the implications for campus governance.* Occasional Paper No. 26. Washington, DC: Association of Governing Boards of Universities and Colleges.

Chait, R. (2000, August 4). Trustees and professors: So often at odds, so much alike. *Chronicle of Higher Education.*

Chambers, G. S. (1999, November 19). Toward shared control of distance education. *Chronicle of Higher Education.*

Chickering, A., and Havinghurst, R. (1981). The life cycle. In A. Chickering and Associates, *The modern American college* (pp. 21–39). San Francisco: Jossey-Bass.

Clampitt, P. G., and DeKoch, R. J. (2001). *Embracing uncertainty: The essence of leadership.* Armonk, NY, and London, Eng.: M. E. Sharpe.

Coble, R. (2000). *Governance and the coordination of public higher education in all 50 states.* Raleigh, NC: Center for Public Policy Research.

Cole, J. (1993). Balancing acts: Dilemmas of choice facing research universities. *Daedalus, 22*(4), 1–7.

Collis, D. (2001). When industries change: The future of higher education. *Continuing Higher Education Review, 65,* 15–32.

Committee T on College and University Government. (1964). Report on the relationship of faculty governance to academic freedom. *Academe, 80*(4).

Cooper, C. I., Cartwright, S., and Early, C. P. (Eds.). (2001). *The international handbook of organizational culture and climate.* New York: Wiley.

Cox, A. M. (2000, November 17). Professors and deans praise shared governance, but criticize corporate model. *Chronicle of Higher Education.*

Davis, J. R. (1993). *Better teaching, more learning: Strategies for success in postsecondary settings.* Phoenix, AZ: ACE/Oryx Press.

de Groof, J., Neave, G., and Svec, J. (1998). *Democracy and governance in higher education.* The Hague, the Netherlands: Kluwer Law International.

de Russy, C. (1996, October 11). Public universities need rigorous oversight by activist trustees. *Chronicle of Higher Education.*

Deal, T. E., and Kennedy, A. A. (1982). *The rites and rituals of corporate life.* Reading, MA: Addison-Wesley.

Dewey, J. (1916). The need of an industrial education in an industrial democracy. *Proceedings of the Second Pan-American Scientific Congress* (Vol. 4), December 27, 1915–January 8, 1916, Washington, DC.

Dickeson, R. C. (1999). Sifting academic priorities. *Trusteeship, 7*(3).

Dolence, M. G., and Norris, D. M. (1994). Using key performance indicators to drive strategic decision making. In V.M.H. Borden and T. W. Banta (Eds.), *Using performance indicators to guide strategic decision making.* New Directions for Institutional Research, no. 82. San Francisco: Jossey-Bass.

Drath, W. H. (2001). *The deep blue sea: Rethinking the source of leadership.* San Francisco: Jossey-Bass.

Durden, W. (2001, October 19). Liberal arts for all, not just the rich. *Chronicle of Higher Education.*

Dykes, A. (1970). *Faculty participation in academic decision-making.* Washington, DC: American Council on Education.

Eckel, P., Hill, B., and Green, M. (1998). *On change: En route to transformation.* Washington, DC: American Council on Education.

Eckel, P., Hill, B., Green, M., and Mallon, W. (1999). *On change. Reports from the road: Insights on institutional change.* Washington, DC: American Council on Education.

Etzkowitz, H., and Stevens, A. J. (1998). Inching toward industrial policy: The university's role in government initiatives to assist small, innovative companies in the United States. In H. Etzkowitz, A. Webster, and P. Healey (Eds.), *Capitalizing knowledge: New intersections of industry and academia.* Albany, NY: State University of New York Press.

Ewell, P. T. (1997, December). Organizing for learning: A new imperative. *AAHE Bulletin.*

Floyd, C. E. (1994). Faculty participation and shared leadership. *Review of Higher Education, 17*(2).

Foster, A. (2002, October 15). Louisiana board of regents shuts down four distance learning institutions. *Chronicle of Higher Education.*

Frances, C., Huxel, G., Meyerson, J., and Park, D. (1987). *Strategic decision making: Key questions and indicators for trustees.* Washington, DC: Association of Governing Boards of Universities and Colleges.

Friedman, A. W. (1996). Good governance. *Academe, 82*(4).

Fujita, E. M. (1990). *What is a good presidential leader? College presidents as seen through the eyes of other campus leaders.* Unpublished Ed.D. dissertation. Teachers College, Columbia University.

Gayle, D. J., Hakim, T. M., Agarwal, V. K., and Alfonso, P. J. (1999). Turning culture clash into collaboration. *Trusteeship, 7*(3), 24–27.

Gentemann, K. M., Fletcher, J. J., and Potter, D.L. (1994). Refocusing the academic program review on student learning: The role of assessment. In M. K. Kinnick (Ed.), *Providing useful information for deans and department chairs* (pp. 31–46). New Directions for Institutional Research, no. 84. San Francisco: Jossey-Bass.

Gerber, L. G. (1997, September–October). Reaffirming the value of shared governance. *Academe,* 7–10.

Gerber, L. G. (2001, May–June). Inextricably linked. *Academe,* 1–3.

Gilmore, T. (1997). The social architecture of group interventions. In J. E. Neumann, K. Kellner, and A. Dawson-Shepherd (Eds.), *Developing Organizational Consultancy.* New York: Routledge.

Glassick, C. E., Huber, M. J., and Maeroff, G. I. (1997). *Scholarship assessed: Evaluation of the professoriate.* San Francisco: Jossey-Bass.

Gleason, B. W. (1991). *Open access: A user information system.* Professional Paper Series CAUSE6. Boulder, CO: National Center for Higher Education Management Systems.

Glenny, L., and Dalglish, T. (1973). *Public universities, state agencies and the law: Constitutional autonomy in decline.* Berkeley: Center for Research and Development in Higher Education, University of California, Berkeley.

Goddard, A. (2003, March 7). 5.5 billion pounds buys single-track universities. *Times Higher Education Supplement.*

Goldman, C. A., Gates, S. M., and Brewer, D. L. (2001, October 5). Prestige or reputation: Which is a sound investment? *Chronicle of Higher Education.*

Gray, P. J. (1991). Using assessment data to improve teaching. In M. Theall and J. Franklin (Eds.), *Effective practices for improving teaching.* New Directions for Teaching and Learning, no 48. San Francisco: Jossey-Bass.

Griffin, R. (1993). Budget cuts and shared governance. *Academe, 79*(6).

Hakim, T. M., Gayle, D. J., Agarwal, V. K., and Alfonso, P. J. (1999). University governance: Perspectives of academic and administrative leaders. *Council of Fellows Newsletter, 21*(2).

Halstead, K. (1989). *State profiles: Financing public higher education, 1978–1989.* Washington, DC: Research Associates.

Hamilton, N. (1999). Are we speaking the same language? Comparing AAUP and AGB. *Liberal Education, 85*(4).

Hamilton, N. (2000). The academic profession's leadership role in shared governance. *Liberal Education, 86*(3), 14–22.

Handy, C. B. (1989). *The age of unreason.* Boston: Harvard Business School Press.

Hanna, D. E. (1998). Higher education in an era of digital competition: Emerging organizational models. *Journal of Asynchronous Learning Networks, 2*(1), 23–35.

Healy, P. (1997, December 19). Leaders of California's 2-year college system say governance structure is at breaking point. *Chronicle of Higher Education.*

Hebel, S. (2003, May 2). Public colleges emphasize research, but the public wants a focus on students. *Chronicle of Higher Education.*

Henderson, A. (1967). Effective models of university governance. In G. K. Smith (Ed.), *Search for leaders: Current issues on higher education.* Washington, DC: American Association for Higher Education.

Hendrickson, R. M., and Bartkovich, J. P. (1986). Organizational systematics: Toward a classificatory scheme for postsecondary institutions. *Review of Higher Education, 9*(3), 12–23.

Heywood, J. (2000). *Assessment in higher education: Student learning, teaching, programmes and institutions.* London and Philadelphia: Jessica Kingsley Publishers.

Hirschorn, L. (1997). *Reworking authority: leading and following in the post-modern organization.* Cambridge, MA: MIT Press.

Hodgkinson, H. L. (1969). "Who decides who decides?" In K. G. Smith (Ed.), *Agony and promise.* San Francisco: Jossey-Bass.

Hodgkinson, H. L. (1971). *Campus governance: The amazing thing is that it works at all.* Washington, DC: ERIC Clearinghouse on Higher Education.

Hodgkinson, H. L., and Meeth, L. R. (1971). *Power and authority: The transformation of campus governance.* San Francisco: Jossey-Bass.

Hollander, E. (1994). Coordinating boards are under attack. *Trusteeship, 2*(4).

Honan, J. P. (1995, Fall). Monitoring institutional performance. *Priorities, 5,* 10–16.

Hooker, M. (1997). The transformation of higher education. In D. G. Oblinger and S. C. Rush (Eds.), *The learning revolution: The challenge of information technology* (pp. 41–62). Boston: Anker.

Howerton, M. (1996, February 21). Shared governance debate arrives at senate. *The Daily Bruin,* University of California at Los Angeles.

Immerwahr, J. (1999). *Taking responsibility: Leaders' expectations of higher education.* Washington, DC: National Center for Public Policy and Higher Education.

Ingram, R. T. (1995). *Effective trusteeship: A guide for board members of independent colleges and universities.* Washington, DC: Association of Governing Boards of Universities and Colleges.

Ingram, R. T. (1999, May 14). Counterpoint. *Chronicle of Higher Education.*

Ingram, R. T. (1999). A reaffirmation, not an attack. *Trusteeship, 7*(3), 8–12.

Jordan, R. (2001). The faculty senate minuet. *Trusteeship, 9*(5), 5–9.

Katchadourian, H., and Boli, J. (1985). *Careerism and intellectualism among college students: Patterns of academic and career choice in the undergraduate years.* San Francisco: Jossey-Bass.

Katz, R. N., and West, R. P. (1992). *Sustaining excellence in the 21st century: A vision and strategies for college and university administration.* Professional Paper Series CAUSE8. Boulder, CO: National Center for Higher Education Management Systems.

Kavanagh, P. (2000). A vision of democratic governance in higher education: The stakes of work in academia. *Social Policy, 30*(24).

Keeton, M. (1977). The constituencies and their claims. In G. L. Riley and J. V. Baldridge (Eds.), *Governing academic organizations* (pp. 194–210). Berkeley, CA: McCutchan.

Keeton, M., and Associates. (1971). *Shared authority on campus.* Washington, DC: American Association for Higher Education.

Keller, G. (Ed.). (1983). *Academic strategy: The management revolution in American higher education.* Baltimore: Johns Hopkins University Press.

Keller, G. (1996). The great American assessment tussle. In *Performance indicators in higher education: What works, what doesn't, and what's next?* (pp. 10–13). Washington, DC: American Association for Higher Education.

Kellogg, A. P. (2001, May 7). Faculty senate, upset at its impotence, may lack power to dissolve itself. *Chronicle of Higher Education.*

Kerr, C., and Gade, M. L. (1989). *The many lives of academic presidents: Time, place and character.* Washington, DC: Association of Governing Boards of Universities and Colleges.

Kezar, A., and Eckel, P. (2000). *Moving beyond the gap between research and practice in higher education.* New Directions for Higher Education, no. 110. San Francisco: Jossey-Bass.

Knight, J. (2002, March 15). *Trends in higher education services: The implications of GATS.* London: Observatory of Borderless Higher Education. [http://www.unesco.org/education/ studyingabroad/highlights/global_forum/gats_he/jk_trade_he_gats_implications.pdf].

Kochan, T. A., and Useem, M. (Eds.). (1992). *Transforming organizations.* New York: Oxford University Press.

Konrad, R. (2001, March 6). E-learning companies look smart even in down market. [http://news.cnet.com/news/0–1007–202–5043194.html].

Larson, W. A. (1994). *When crisis strikes on campus.* New York: CASE Books.

Layzell, D. T. (1992, February 19). Tight budgets demand studies of faculty productivity. *Chronicle of Higher Education.*

Layzell, D. T., and Lyddon, J. W. (1990). *Budgeting for higher education at the state level: Enigma, paradox and ritual.* ASHE-ERIC Higher Education Report, no. 4. Washington, DC: School of Education and Human Development, George Washington University.

Leatherman, C. (1998a, January 9). NRLB may end its opposition to unions for private college professors. *Chronicle of Higher Education.*

Leatherman, C. (1998b, January 30). Shared governance under siege: Is it time to revive it or get rid of it? *Chronicle of Higher Education.*

Leatherman, C. (1999, July 9). Contract talks and civility break down at Miami-Dade: Governance issues divide the faculty from the president at an influential community college. *Chronicle of Higher Education.*

Leatherman, C. (2000, January 21). Union movement at private colleges awakens after a 20-year slumber. *Chronicle of Higher Education.*

Lee, R. J., and King, S. N. (2001). How changing realities and perceptions affect you as a leader. *Leadership in Action, 21*(1), 15–29.

Levine, A. (1997). How the academic profession is changing. *Daedalus, 26*(4), 4–7.

Loevinger, J. (1976). *Ego development: Conceptions and theories.* San Francisco: Jossey-Bass.

Longanecker, D. A. (2001). The public-private balance: Keeping higher education's reason for being in perspective. *AAHE Bulletin, 53*(9), 3–4.

Lucas, C. J. (1994). *American higher education: A history.* New York: St. Martin's Press.

Macedo, S. (1990). *Liberal virtues.* Oxford, Eng.: Clarendon Press.

Magner, D. K. (1999, June 18). Battle over academic control pits faculty against governing board at George Mason University. *Chronicle of Higher Education.*

Magner, D. K. (2000, May 19). George Mason University faculty votes to censure board for interfering with curriculum. *Chronicle of Higher Education.*

Makar, S. D. (2002, November 8). Litigious students and academic disputes. *Chronicle of Higher Education.*

Marcus, L. R. (1999, September–October). Democracy and the academy. *On the Horizon,* 5–11.

Massy, W. F., Wilger, A. K., and Colbeck, C. (1994). Overcoming hollowed collegiality. *Change, 20*(2), 6–11.

McConnell, T. R. (1970). *Campus governance and faculty participation.* Berkeley, CA: Center for Research and Development in Higher Education. (ED 039844)

Meyers, R. T. (1994). *Strategic budgeting*. Ann Arbor: University of Michigan Press.

Michaelson, M. (1998). Rising to the defense of faculty. *Trusteeship, 6*(1).

Miller, M. A. (1998). *Campus governance*. Paper presented at the Annual Conference of the American Association for Higher Education, June 20–23, Atlanta, GA.

Miller, M. T. (1996). *The faculty forum: A case study in shared authority*. Tuscaloosa: University of Alabama. (ED 401 774)

Miller, M. T., McCormack, T. F., Maddox, J. F., and Seagren, A. T. (1996). Faculty participation in governance at small and large universities: Implications for practice. *Planning and Changing, 27*(3–4), 12–23.

Millett, J. D. (1962). *The academic community*. New York: McGraw-Hill.

Millett, J. D. (1980). *Management, governance and leadership: A guide for college and university administrators*. New York: AMACOM.

National Association of College and University Business Officers. (1997, October). Xers show commitment to higher education and technology, survey shows. *Business Officer*.

National Association of College and University Business Officers. (2001). *The cost of higher education*. Washington, DC: National Association of College and University Business Officers.

National Center for Education Statistics. (1997). *Digest of Education Statistics*. Washington, DC: U.S. Department of Education.

National Center for Postsecondary Improvement. (2001a). A report to stakeholders on the condition and effectiveness of postsecondary education. Part 1: The recent college graduate. *Change, 33*(3), 11–17.

National Center for Postsecondary Improvement. (2001b). A report to stakeholders on the condition and effectiveness of postsecondary education. Part 2: The public. *Change, 33*(3), 8–15.

National Center for Postsecondary Improvement. (2002). A report to stakeholders on the condition and effectiveness of postsecondary education. Part 3: Employers. *Change, 34*(1), 1–9.

National Labor Relations Board v. *Yeshiva University,* 103 LRRM 2526 (1980).

Nelson, C. (1999, April 16). The war against the faculty. *Chronicle of Higher Education*.

Newman, F. (2000). Saving higher education's soul. *Change, 33*(5), 5–11.

Newton, R. R. (2000, Winter). For-profit and traditional institutions: What can be learned from the differences? *The Academic Workplace,* 4–7.

Oblinger, D. G., and Rush, S. C. (2000). *The learning revolution: The challenge of information technology in the academy*. Boston: Anker.

O'Neil, R. M. (2001). What we mean by academic freedom. *Trusteeship, 9*(5), 8–14.

Pascarella, E. T. (2001, May–June). Identifying excellence in undergraduate education: Are we even close? *Change,* 5–12.

Payette, D. L. (2001). What we mean by fiduciary responsibility. *Trusteeship, 9*(5), 6-11.

Peterson, M. W., and Mets, L. A. (1987). *Key resources on higher education governance, management and leadership: A guide to the literature*. San Francisco: Jossey-Bass.

Pew Higher Education Roundtable. (1995, June). *New challenges to academic governance*. New York: Pew.

Press, E., and Washburn, J. (2000, March). The kept university. *Atlantic Monthly,* 4–9.

Pritchett, H. S. (1905, September). Shall the university become a business corporation? *Atlantic Monthly,* 6–10.

Pulley, J. (2002, December 20). Independent report generally clears auburn university of charges that it acted inappropriately. *Chronicle of Higher Education.*

Pusser, B., and Doane, D. (2001, September/October). Public purpose and private enterprise: The contemporary organization of postsecondary education. *Change, 5–9.*

Rice, E. R., and Austin, A. E. (1988). High faculty morale. *Change, 20*(2), 7–12.

Richardson, J. T. (1999a). Big, bad governance. *Trusteeship, 7*(3), 14–19.

Richardson, J. T. (1999b, February 12). Centralizing governance isn't simply wrong: It's bad business too. *Chronicle of Higher Education.*

Richardson, R., Bracco, K. R., Callan, P., and Finney, J. (1998). *Higher education governance: Balancing institutional and market influences.* Washington, DC: National Center for Public Policy and Higher Education.

Richardson, W. D., and Rickman, D. K. (1998). Democracy's quarrel with the academy: A view from the ramparts. *Policy Studies Review, 15*(4), 22–31.

Riley, G. L., and Baldridge, J. V. (1977). *Governing academic organizations.* Berkeley, CA: McCutchan.

Rojstaczer, S. (1999). *Gone for good: Tales of university life after the golden age.* Oxford, Eng., and New York: Oxford University Press.

Rokeach, M. (1973). *The nature of human values.* New York: Free Press.

Rosenzweig, R. M. (1994). The permeable university: Academic life in an age of special interests. *Interchange, 25*(1).

Ross, J. E., and Halstead, C. P. (2001). *Public relations and the presidency: Strategies and tactics for effective communications.* New York: CASE Books.

Ruderman, M. N., and Rogolsky, S. (2001). Getting real: How to lead authentically. *Leadership in Action, 21*(3), 9–17.

Sample, S. B. (2001, October 19). When the buck stops, think contrarily. *Chronicle of Higher Education.*

Sanderson, A. V., Phua, C., and Herda, D. (2000). *The American faculty poll.* Chicago: National Opinion Research Center.

Schein, E. H. (1992). *Organizational culture and leadership.* San Francisco: Jossey-Bass.

Schick, E. G., Novak, R. J., Norton, J. A., and Elam, H. G. (1993). *Shared visions of public education governance: Structures and leadership styles that work.* Washington, DC: Association of Governing Boards of Universities and Colleges.

Schmidt, P. (1999, July 2). A state transforms colleges with "performance funding." *Chronicle of Higher Education.*

Schmidt, P. (2002, October 1). Competition endangers colleges' commitment to public, study says. *Chronicle of Higher Education.*

Schneider, A. (2000, November 24). Four professors win top national prize for college teaching. *Chronicle of Higher Education,* A10.

Schoenfeld, C., and Weimer, L., with Lang, J. M. (1997). *Reaching out: How academic leaders can communicate more effectively with their constituencies.* New York: CASE Books.

Scott, J. (1997, November–December). Death by inattention: The strange fate of faculty governance. *Academe,* 4–7.

Sevier, R. A. (2000). *Strategic planning in higher education: Theory and practice.* New York: CASE Books.

Sinfonis, J. G., and Goldberg, B. (1996). *Corporation on a tightrope: Balancing leadership, governance and technology in an age of complexity.* New York: Oxford University Press.

Sowell, T. (1994, February 14). Power without responsibility. *Forbes,* 15–26.

Spence, L. D. (2001, November-December). The case against teaching. *Change,* 6–10.

Splete, A. P., and Dickeson, R. C. (2001). Five boards that lit a spark. *Trusteeship, 9*(1), 14–22.

Springer, M. (2001). The future of the professoriate: How can we address the needs of future faculty and the demands of higher education? *Fellows Newsletter, 23*(1), 2–3.

Suggs, W. (2001, April 19). Auburn University trustees have usurped control of athletics, former president says. *Chronicle of Higher Education.*

Terenzini, P. T. (1993). On the nature of institutional research and the knowledge and skills it requires. *Research in Higher Education, 34*(1), 12–19.

Thomas, Q. (1998). *Trends in governance and management of higher education.* Washington, DC: The World Bank, Human Development Department, Latin American and the Caribbean Regional Office.

Tierney, W. G. (1998). *The responsive university.* Baltimore: Johns Hopkins University Press.

Trevino, L. (1990). A cultural perspective on changing and developing organizational ethics. *Research on Organizational Change and Development, 4,* 195–230.

Trow, M. (1997, May 16). The chiefs of public universities should be civil servants, not political actors. *Chronicle of Higher Education.*

Tuckman, B. W. (1994). Assessing effective teaching. *Peabody Journal of Education,* Nashville, Tennessee: George Peabody College for Teachers.

Twale, D. J., and Shannon, D. M. (1996). Gender differences among faculty in campus governance: Nature of involvement, satisfaction and power. *Initiatives, 57*(4).

U.S. Census Bureau. (1998). [http://www.census.gov].

Van Dusen, G. C. (1997). *The virtual campus: Technology and reform in higher education.* ASHE-ERIC Higher Education Report, vol. 25 no. 5. Washington, DC: George Washington University, Graduate School of Education and Human Development.

Victor, B., and Cullen, J. (1988). The organizational bases of ethical work climates. *Administrative Science Quarterly, 33,* 101–125.

Ward, D. (2003, Winter). Strategic planning at ACE: Guiding a venerable institution forward into a new century. *The Presidency,* 18–23.

Webber, A. (1997, May). Learning for a change. *Fast Company.*

Wergin, J. F., and McMillan, J. H. (1998). Understanding and evaluating education research. Upper Saddle River, NJ: Merrill.

West, J. A., Seidata, V., di Mattia, J., and Whalen, E. L. (1997, August). RCM as a catalyst: Study examines use of responsibility center management on campus. *Business Officer,* 4–9.

Whalen, E. L. (1991). *Responsibility center budgeting: An approach to decentralized management for institutions of higher education.* Bloomington and Indianapolis: Indiana University Press.

Wilber, K. (1998). *The marriage of sense and soul: Integrating science and religion.* New York: Random House.

Will, T. E. (1901, September). A menace to freedom: The college trust. *Arena, 26,* 8–17.

Wilson, E. B. (2001). Bridge-Building 101. *Trusteeship, 9*(2), 10–14.

Winston, G. C. (1997). Why can't a college be more like a firm?" *Change, 29*(5), 5–9.

Wohlstetter, P., and Van Kirk, A. (1995). *School-based budgeting: Organizing for high performance.* Los Angeles: Center on Educational Governance, University of Southern California.

Wolfe, A. (1996). The feudal culture of the postmodern university. *The Wilson Quarterly, 20*(1).

Yammarino, F. J., and Dansereau, F. (2001). A multiple-level approach for understanding the nature of leadership studies. In C. L. Outcalt, S. K. Faris, and K. N. McMahon (Eds.), *Developing non-hierarchical leadership on campus: Case studies and best practices in higher education* (pp. 24–37). Westport, CT: Greenwood Press.

Zemsky, R., Shannon, S., and Shapiro, D. B. (2001). Higher education as a competitive enterprise: When markets matter. San Francisco: Jossey-Bass.

Zumeta, W. (1998). Public university accountability to the state in the late twentieth century: Time for a rethinking? *Policy Studies Review, 15*(4), 22–35.

Name Index

A

Agarwal, V. K., 4, 34
Alfonso, P. J., 4, 34
Altbach, P. G., 3
Argyris, C., 75
Armstrong, L., 50
Astin, A. W., 4, 18
Auden, W. H., 47
Austin, A. E., 76

B

Baez, B., 50
Baker, B., 81
Baldridge, J. V., 16, 51
Barak, R., 38, 39
Barrazone, E., 26
Barrow, C. W., 45
Bartkovich, J. P., 28
Basinger, J., 30, 52
Bates, A. W., 91
Baucus, M., 43
Bellow, S., 48
Benjamin, R., ix, 65
Bennis, W., 30, 47
Berube, M., 94
Bess, J. L., 42
Biggs, J., 74, 75, 77
Birnbaum, R., 17, 21, 27, 28, 54, 55, 108
Blimling, G. S., 75
Boli, J., 79
Bolman, L. G., 29
Bowen, R., 44

Bowie, N. E., 15
Boyer, E. L., 70
Braithwaite, J., 43
Bransten, L., 87
Breslin, R., 73, 74
Brewer, D. L., 20
Bronfenbrenner, K., 52
Brown, M., 17
Brown, S., 75
Brown, W. O., Jr., 51
Brownstein, A., 52
Brubacher, J. S., 22
Burke, J. C., 36
Burnside, R. M., 83
Buttrick, W., 45

C

Callan, P. M., 35, 60, 63, 65
Carnevale, D., 91, 93
Carroll, S., ix, 65
Cartwright, S., 76
Case, J., 101
Centra, J. A., 50
Chait, R., 34, 43, 70
Chambers, G. S., 93
Chickering, A., 79
Clampitt, P. G., 26
Coble, R., 39
Colbeck, C., 76
Cole, J., 29, 42
Collis, D., 14, 15
Cooper, C. I., 76
Cox, A. M., 50

Subject Index

Dennis J. Gayle is senior advisor to the vice chancellor and professor of strategic international business at the University of the West Indies, St. Augustine, Trinidad. He was educated at the University of the West Indies' Mona campus, Oxford University, the London School of Economics and Political Science, and the University of California at Los Angeles. Professor Gayle has served in several capitals and participated in a range of major international economic conferences as a senior diplomatic officer. He was a 1997–1998 Fellow of the American Council of Education, and a 2001 graduate of Harvard University's Institute of Educational Management. He has also served as associate vice president for academic affairs at the University of North Florida. His publications include many books, book chapters, and journal articles.

Bhoendradatt Tewarie is principal and vice chancellor of the University of the West Indies, St. Augustine, Trinidad. He formerly served as executive director of the Institute of Business, as a cabinet minister responsible for industry, enterprise, and tourism in the government of Trinidad and Tobago, and as chairman of the National Institute for Higher Education, Research, Science and Technology (NIHURST). At NIHURST he led the creation of Trinidad and Tobago's first national community college. He is currently seeking to bring a more business-like approach to university administration at the University of the West Indies as the institution embarks on a strategic transformation.

A. Quinton White, Jr., is professor of marine science at Jacksonville University in Florida, where he established the major in marine science, served as department chair and chair of the Division of Science and Mathematics, and served as dean of the College of Arts and Sciences. Professor White received his Ph.D. from the University of South Carolina, M.S. from University of Virginia, and B.S. from North Carolina Wesleyan College. His has been active in marine science education with research concerning the human impact on the marine ecosystems. He was Jacksonville's Professor of the Year in 1988. In 1997, he was named American Council on Education Fellow and spent a year as assistant to the provost at Elon College, NC. He has been active in various civic organizations and developed an interest in leadership and faculty governance.

About the ASHE-ERIC
Higher Education Reports Series

Since 1983, the ASHE-ERIC Higher Education Report Series has been providing researchers, scholars, and practitioners with timely and substantive information on the critical issues facing higher education. Each monograph presents a definitive analysis of a higher education problem or issue, based on a thorough synthesis of significant literature and institutional experiences. Topics range from planning to diversity and multiculturalism, to performance indicators, to curricular innovations. The mission of the Series is to link the best of higher education research and practice to inform decision making and policy. The reports connect conventional wisdom with research and are designed to help busy individuals keep up with the higher education literature. Authors are scholars and practitioners in the academic community. Each report includes an executive summary, review of the pertinent literature, descriptions of effective educational practices, and a summary of key issues to keep in mind to improve educational policies and practice.

The Series is one of the most peer reviewed in higher education. A National Advisory Board made up of ASHE members reviews proposals. A National Review Board of ASHE scholars and practitioners reviews completed manuscripts. Six monographs are published each year and they are approximately 120 pages in length. The reports are widely disseminated through Jossey-Bass and John Wiley & Sons, and they are available online to subscribing institutions through Wiley InterScience (http://www.interscience.wiley.com).

Call for Proposals

The ASHE-ERIC Higher Education Report Series is actively looking for proposals. We encourage you to contact the editor, Dr. Adrianna Kezar, at kezar@usc.edu with your ideas. For detailed information about the Series, please visit http://www.eriche.org/publications/writing.html.

Recent Titles

Volume 29 ASHE-ERIC Higher Education Reports

1. Ensuring Quality and Productivity in Higher Education:
   An Analysis of Assessment Practices
   Susan M. Gates and Associates

2. Institutionalizing a Broader View of Scholarship Through Boyer's Four Domains
   John M. Braxton, William Luckey, and Patricia Helland

3. Transforming the Curriculum: Preparing Students for a Changing World
   Elizabeth A. Jones

4. Quality in Distance Education: Focus on On-Line Learning
   Katrina A. Meyer

5. Faculty Service Roles and the Scholarship of Engagement
   Kelly Ward

6. Identity Development of Diverse Populations: Implications for Teaching and
   Administration in Higher Education
   Vasti Torres, Mary F. Howard-Hamilton, Diane L. Cooper

Volume 28 ASHE-ERIC Higher Education Reports

1. The Changing Nature of the Academic Deanship
   Mimi Wolverton, Walter H. Gmelch, Joni Montez, and Charles T. Nies

2. Faculty Compensation Systems: Impact on the Quality of Higher Education
   Terry P. Sutton, Peter J. Bergerson

3. Socialization of Graduate and Professional Students in Higher Education:
   A Perilous Passage?
   John C. Weidman, Darla J. Twale, Elizabeth Leahy Stein

4. Understanding and Facilitating Organizational Change in the 21st Century: Recent
   Research and Conceptualizations
   Adrianna J. Kezar

5. Cost Containment in Higher Education: Issues and Recommendations
   Walter A. Brown, Cayo Gamber

6. Facilitating Students' Collaborative Writing
   Bruce W. Speck

Back Issue/Subscription Order Form

Copy or detach and send to:

Jossey-Bass, A Wiley Company, 989 Market Street, San Francisco CA 94103-1741

Call or fax toll-free: Phone 888-378-2537 6:30AM – 3PM PST; Fax 888-481-2665

Back Issues: Please send me the following issues at $24 each
(Important: please include series abbreviation and issue number.
For example AEHE28:1)

_____

_____

_____

$ _____   Total for single issues

$ _____   SHIPPING CHARGES: SURFACE   Domestic Canadian
                                    First Item $5.00 $6.00
                                    Each Add'l Item $3.00 $1.50
                 For next-day and second-day delivery rates, call the number listed above.

Subscriptions   Please ❑ start ❑ renew my subscription to *ASHE-ERIC Higher
                Education Reports for the year 2_____at the following rate:

                U.S.   ❑ Individual $165   ❑ Institutional $165
                Canada   ❑ Individual $165   ❑ Institutional $225
                All Others   ❑ Individual $213   ❑ Institutional $276
                Online Subscription   ❑ Institutional $150

                **For more information about online subscriptions visit
                www.interscience.wiley.com**

$ _____   Total single issues and subscriptions (Add appropriate sales tax
                 for your state for single issue orders. No sales tax for U.S.
                 subscriptions. Canadian residents, add GST for subscriptions and
                 single issues.)

❑Payment enclosed (U.S. check or money order only)
❑VISA ❑ MC ❑ AmEx _____ Exp. Date _____

Signature _____ Day Phone _____
❑ Bill Me (U.S. institutional orders only. Purchase order required.)

Purchase order # _____
                 Federal Tax ID13559302   GST 89102 8052

Name _____

Address _____

_____

Phone _____ E-mail _____

For more information about Jossey-Bass, visit our Web site at www.josseybass.com

PROMOTION CODE ND03

**ASHE-ERIC HIGHER EDUCATION REPORT
IS NOW AVAILABLE ONLINE AT WILEY INTERSCIENCE**

What is Wiley InterScience?

Wiley InterScience is the dynamic online content service from John Wiley &
Sons delivering the full text of over 300 leading scientific, technical, medical,
and professional journals, plus major reference works, the acclaimed Current
Protocols laboratory manuals, and even the full text of select Wiley print books
online.

What are some special features of Wiley InterScience?

Wiley Interscience Alerts is a service that delivers table of contents via e-mail
for any journal available on Wiley InterScience as soon as a new issue is
published online.
Early View is Wiley's exclusive service presenting individual articles online as
soon as they are ready, even before the release of the compiled print issue.
These articles are complete, peer-reviewed, and citable.
CrossRef is the innovative multi-publisher reference linking system enabling
readers to move seamlessly from a reference in a journal article to the cited
publication, typically located on a different server and published by a different
publisher.

How can I access Wiley InterScience?

Visit http://www.interscience.wiley.com.

Guest Users can browse Wiley InterScience for unrestricted access to journal
Tables of Contents and Article Abstracts, or use the powerful search engine.
Registered Users are provided with a *Personal Home Page* to store and
manage customized alerts, searches, and links to favorite journals and articles.
Additionally, Registered Users can view free Online Sample Issues and preview
selected material from major reference works.
Licensed Customers are entitled to access full-text journal articles in PDF, with
select journals also offering full-text HTML.

How do I become an Authorized User?

Authorized Users are individuals authorized by a paying Customer to have
access to the journals in Wiley InterScience. For example, a University that
subscribes to Wiley journals is considered to be the Customer.
Faculty, staff and students authorized by the University to have access to those
journals in Wiley InterScience are Authorized Users. Users should contact their
Library for information on which Wiley journals they have access to in
Wiley InterScience.

ASK YOUR INSTITUTION ABOUT WILEY INTERSCIENCE TODAY!